D0378891

# THE
# MEDICAL
# INDUSTRIAL
# COMPLEX

# THE
# MEDICAL
# INDUSTRIAL
# COMPLEX

## STANLEY WOHL, M.D.

Harmony Books, New York

For my late father, Benny Wohl,
and for the late Hugh S. Cohen

Published by Harmony Books, a division of Crown Publishers, Inc., One Park Avenue, New York, New York 10016 and simultaneously in Canada by General Publishing Company Limited.

HARMONY and colophon are trademarks of Crown Publishers, Inc.

Manufactured in the United States of America

Library of Congress Cataloging in Publication Data

Wohl, Stanley
   The medical-industrial complex.
   1. Medical care, Cost of—United States.   2. Health facilities, Proprietary—United States.   3. Medical corporations—United States.   I. Title.
RA410.53.W64   1984      338.4'73621'0973      83-26509
ISBN 0-517-55351-1

10  9  8  7  6  5  4  3  2  1

First Edition

# CONTENTS

# NOTE

To avoid clumsiness, the many numbers and statistics in this book have not been individually footnoted. The extensive bibliography at the back of this volume substantiates all information used. For the most part, the statistics concerning companies have been obtained from their own annual reports and 10K reports to the Securities and Exchange Commission, all of which are public records.

The statistics concerning physicians and hospitals were taken primarily from federal publications originating in the Office of Management and Budget, the Bureau of the Census, the Department of Commerce, the Department of Health and Human Services; also consulted were the American Medical Asociation monthly and annual reports. The figures are accurate as of late 1983.

# 1
# THE UNKINDEST CUT

Ethics cannot be one-sided. If the physicians have moral obligations to society, there should be reciprocal obligations of society
toward the physicians.

—LESTER S. KING, M.D.
*Journal of the American Medical
Association* (1982)

This book tells the story of the explosive growth of a major new
American industry, corporate medicine. It chronicles the spectacular rise of a large number of Wall Street–listed companies
that have in the last few years become giant health care
providers on a national scale, and it recounts the recent activity
of some of the older, better known corporate health suppliers.
The high profit performance of both the new providers and the
traditional suppliers—and some hybrid conglomerates that
deal in the two services—signals the arrival in this country of
health care as a corporate endeavor, competing side by side
with other lucrative ventures for investment dollars throughout
the land. Indeed, in America, the transition of the practice of
medicine from a science and art dedicated to the preservation

1

of life to a boardroom activity in pursuit of shareholder profits is virtually complete. The personal, social, economic, and political implications of the new arrangement promise to be immense.

In the first part of the book I relate some of the history and the ramifications of corporate medicine as it is now practiced, and I also try to be specific, and somewhat objective, about the dangers and virtues of the new system. In the chapter called "Some of the Players," I present detailed information on some thirty-five (and an accompanying table of one hundred) of the leading companies involved in one way or another in the health care industry—their activities, their financing, their manner of doing business, their often reciprocally beneficial interrelations. In the last chapter, I offer some suggestions on how the country might avoid, essentially by means of stricter regulations, what I perceive to be the greatest perils of the medicine-corporation merger.

While I strongly criticize some of the activities of big business, I also clearly recognize their positive contribution and the fact that they must be included in any scheme for reforming the system. If one approaches the matter from a neutral ideological position, one can probably see both the beneficial and the adverse consequences of, as well as a certain hindsight inevitability to, the new manner of health care delivery. On the credit side, for example, the for-profit systems claim to be working toward cost containment and uniform standards. On the debit side, the for-profit companies practice deliberate overutilization and choose, when they are free to choose, affluent patients and high-mark-up treatments only.

But it is also true that some doctors have come a far way all by themselves toward acting (and being perceived by the public as acting) very differently from the selfless apostles of cure and healing they thought themselves to be. In many ways the medical profession itself directly and indirectly abetted the for-profit takeover of its sacred calling. In other ways, the advent of expensive medical technologies made further consolidations, in the absence of a clear government policy, unavoidable. At any rate, in the United States since the 1970s, the pattern prevailed for better or worse that powerfully moneyed corporations, with their own rules and values, have turned their acquisitive attention to the health care field—possibly because it was in trouble, possibly because it was seen as a sure money maker, possibly for both these reasons—as they did to other fields, such as book publishing and entertainment, that had earlier eluded their homogenizing grasp.

Evidence of the growing corporate dominance is everywhere. Pick up a magazine that carries glossy ads, and you will see a full-color photograph of a wistful-looking woman in her thirties, wearing dancing tights. Her overall appearance lends a palpable persuasiveness to the copy that invites her to look carefully at her body—her falling buttocks, her flabby thighs, her sagging breasts, her aging face—and to do something about it. The ad is copyrighted by one of the large hospital corporations, Humana Inc. The corporation, it would seem, is seeking more revenue from one of its underutilized operating rooms by playing, as ads have always played, on the weaknesses and insecurities of frail humanity. But this time it's not a cosmetic or a mouthwash that's being hawked—it's invasive surgery that, even under conditions of necessity, should not be lightly undertaken. But corporate practice calls for each branch of the "operation" (the appropriate word here) to earn its share of profits. Staff surgeons must cut; hospital beds must be filled. Besides, who can really hold a corporation responsible for what an individual freely chooses to do? The surgery, when it takes place, will in every way be voluntary.

For more evidence of the far-reaching corporate hand, visit the huge shopping mall a couple of miles outside the city, convenient to a number of well-to-do suburban towns. Alongside the inviting shops selling expensive dresses, gourmet foods, electronic equipment, and joggers' togs is a spanking new storefront, with an eye-catching logo announcing a corporate-owned clinic, MedFirst, franchised like Burger King, and dispensing walk-in medicine. The clinic, with its staff of hired physicians working by the hour, answers an obvious need. Doctors for the most part have stopped making house calls, and when they do they charge large fees. Here then, courtesy of the corporation, is a practical alternative—a reliable (though it may only be open business hours) and reasonably priced (but then you may only get what you pay for) health care facility. Pretty soon every shopping center will have one.

A further sign is reflected in the story told to me by a physician friend, a competent internist who contracted to rent office space in a Houston medical building associated with a nearby chain hospital. The understanding was that the doctor would refer his patients to the company hospital and make use of the company's facilities for medical tests, X-rays, and so on. The arrangement seemed beneficial all around. After all, there are things that the company does better than the doctor—renting, billing, and managing expensive medical equipment, for example. But two years later the physician was confronted with a punitive raise in rent. He had been made to understand that the corporate executives had not been pleased with the small number of patients he had admitted to the hospital—a physician's badge of honor in any other circumstances—or with the small volume of tests he had ordered. He was now encouraged to leave the glamorous office in the corporation building and hang his shingle elsewhere.

Or consider the case of another physician living in Los Angeles, who was interested in forming an association with a new chain hospital on the outskirts of the city. Again, the hospital itself was a gleaming affair—the perfect place, or so it seemed, in which to be sick or practice medicine. Upon entering the facility on an exploratory visit, the physician asked to be taken to the head of the hospital. He was promptly introduced to the hospital administrator, a public relations executive. When the physician told that gentleman that he wished rather to see the head of the medical staff in order to learn something of the hospital's practices, the administrator replied, "Sir, *I* am the head of the medical staff."

The corporations are here, and in all likelihood they are here to stay. And one way or another they have brought the idea of profit—shareholder profit, speculator profit—into the medical domain. It is certainly not a new concept (the rich and powerful drug companies have been with us all along), but it is one that, in its new outfit, I find difficult to accept. Ironically, one of the questions that motivated me to write this book came from a stockbroker who asked, "How is it that so many great university and public hospitals—McLean, Bellevue, Stanford—are going bankrupt while the hospital chains are making a fortune?" As a stock market expert he knew that the shares of the new medical corporations had become, with minimal publicity, the hottest stocks on Wall Street. Just how the corporations have managed over the last few years to find gold while the other prospectors lost their shirts, along with some of their dignity, reveals some of the fundamental operating principles behind the new Medical Industrial Complex.

If I display a bias in relating this story it is that of a physician with a strong appreciation for the rich history and traditions of my profession. I also have great respect for profit-making enterprises and, indeed, have myself participated in some corporate ventures. Not one to bite the hand that feeds, I acknowledge that I made my way through medical school and purchased my first home with money I made on the stock market. In fact, this book began as a research project for a major brokerage firm desiring a fuller understanding of the

5

explosive growth of health care corporations. Much of the factual material I present in this work was obtained in personal interviews with senior executives of some of the companies I discuss—very competent businessmen whom I greatly admire.

I emerged from those interviews with my faith in business and my faith in medicine separately intact, but with an even stronger belief that an unregulated business-medicine marriage spelled disaster for the moral and ethical foundations of the latter. One would just as soon stand idly by while the money changers, who might be most welcome and helpful elsewhere, took over the administration of religion.

Medicine concerns the inalienable right of each individual to enjoy the healthiest, most disease-free body that state-of-the-art knowledge allows. In its commitment to that right, the practice of medicine has stood apart from the values of the marketplace. I fear that the unfettered corporate practice of medicine may well destroy that commitment.

# 2
# THE MEDICAL MOGULS

There are ethical considerations where the historic direct relationship between patient and physician is involved which are
quite different than the usual considerations prevailing in ordi-
nary commercial matters.

—JUSTICE ROBERT H. JACKSON
U.S. Supreme Court (1952)

In the late 1950s, a Nashville cardiologist by the name of
Thomas Frist, Sr., fed up with the sorry state of the city's
hospitals, took the initiative to start up a facility of his own, the
Park View Hospital. A few years later, unable to raise the
money needed for what he saw as the necessary expansion of his
operation, Frist and some fellow physicians took the unusual—
and, as it turned out, historically significant—step of selling
shares in the hospital in order to raise capital.

At about the same time that Park View went public, a
Mormon accountant from Utah named Roy E. Christensen
incorporated the three nursing homes he owned in Pasadena,
California, under the name of Beverly Enterprises. While Frist
concentrated his corporate efforts only on his one hospital,

Christensen involved Beverly in such diverse activities as the manufacture of mirrors and real estate development.

The year 1965 is a watershed year in this story. As part of Lyndon Johnson's Great Society legislation, the U.S. Congress passed the Medicare and Medicaid entitlement programs for the elderly and poor of the country (Medicare basically pays medical costs for the elderly and the young; Medicaid pays these costs for the poor and destitute and disabled of any age). The legislation was admirable and well meaning, but in many ways it was badly flawed. In exchange for short-term political advantage it promised more than it could deliver. The advice of the experts who predicted rapidly escalating health costs for the future was totally ignored. And the predicted occurred.

Corporate accountants as well as individual doctors quickly realized that the Medicare and Medicaid reimbursement schedules were generous in the extreme. The possibility of amassing astronomical profits from running a high-volume, cost-efficient operation was clear from the start. It comes as no surprise, then, to find that these government programs perked the interest of business investors and speculators who liked the idea of having, as a client, an entity as reliable and affluent as the federal government. The development of the so-called Medicare mills in the early 1970s, mostly in the states of New York and New Jersey, constitutes perhaps the sorriest episode in the history of this well-intentioned legislation. And, given the politically charged nature of Medicare and Medicaid, it was all but impossible, at the time, to revoke or revise their more ill-conceived features.

While the problems with the new programs were becoming more and more evident, Thomas Frist's Park View Hospital was thriving. Observing his success, the proprietors of a number of hospitals in the state of Tennessee asked Frist for help in raising capital to gear up—to put it bluntly—for the expected influx of Medicare and Medicaid dollars. To his credit, the doctor quickly realized the advantage, in the new Medicare era, of stringing together several hospitals in order to combine administrative and other functions. In 1968 Frist, together with his son, Thomas Frist, Jr., and an ex-patient of his, Jack Massey (one of the founders, by the way, of the Kentucky Fried Chicken empire), founded the Hospital Corporation of America. Within just six months the new corporation came to control eleven hospitals; in the next fifteen years it would be running close to four hundred.

At about the same time another medical corporation was born in Louisville, Kentucky, through efforts of two farsighted entrepreneurs, Wendell Cherry and David Jones. Called the Humana Corporation, it started with $4 million in cash and ownership of a few local nursing homes. In 1969, in order to cash in on the windfall profits available as a result of Medicare legislation, Humana began selling its nursing homes, while buying and building hospitals instead. Fifteen years later the company would be realizing revenues of $1,516 million per year.

In the same year, 1969, Richard K. Eamer, John C. Bedrosian, and Leonard Cohen, three lawyers, formed National Medical Enterprises in Los Angeles, California. Eamer's law practice included representation of a number of hospitals, four of which required funds for expansion that traditional channels no longer seemed able to furnish. With one eye on Medicare and one ear to the ground, Eamer and his fellow lawyers elected to follow Thomas Frist's example and establish a corporation that could tap Wall Street capital.

The stories of the founders of Hospital Corporation of America, Humana, and National Medical Enterprises were to be repeated by several other medical entrepreneurs, such as Lifemark's Mackey and Frison in Houston and American Medical International's Diener and Weissman in Beverly Hills. The formula in all cases was very nearly the same: study the

9

Medicare legislation; form a corporation; go public to raise capital; acquire more and more health care facilities; and make a healthy profit for all concerned.

Most of the better known acute care (hospitals or other facilities set up for short-term intensive medical treatment) corporations came into being sometime between 1965 and 1970 and have grown by acrobatic leaps and bounds ever since. On the other hand, the original Medicare and Medicaid legislation did not seem so kind to the *chronic* care (nursing homes set up for long-term maintenance and care) facilities (except when they were run in the notorious Medicare mill fashion), and the nursing home industry headed for an early shake-out. In 1971 a chemical engineer by the name of Robert Van Tuyle became the director of Beverly Enterprises. In 1973 Beverly went into the red for the first time in its short history and the entire corporate health care world trembled; for here was a significant and perhaps prophetic hint of trouble in what had up till now been a sea of smooth sailing. But between 1973 and 1977, with everyone watching, Van Tuyle carried out radical surgery on Beverly and turned the company's fortunes around. He settled numerous lawsuits having to do with its seemingly certain bankruptcy and went on to accomplish a major coup. Suffering from financial woes and fearing that National Medical Enterprises' Hillhaven Corporation would attempt a takeover, Van Tuyle nevertheless was able to persuade Stephen's Inc., one of the largest investment firms in the South, to buy a large block of Beverly's unissued preferred stock.

The move neatly headed off the Hillhaven bid and furnished Beverly with a much needed $2.8 million in cash. One year later Stephen's Inc. sold Beverly Enterprises its own hefty nursing home chain, a transaction that doubled Beverly's size and overnight made it the number two corporation—second only to Hillhaven—in the industry. At the same time, David R. Banks left Stephen's Inc. to become president of Beverly

Enterprises. Together Van Tuyle and Banks launched Beverly on an acquisition program that soon made it the leading owner of nursing homes in the country, the position it retains to this day.

The 1975–1976 corporate maneuverings of Van Tuyle and Banks were viewed by many at the time as the dying gasps of desperate operators. The industry itself was seen to be floundering—indeed many financial analysts expected the entire health care house of cards to come tumbling down, sending the once overconfident speculators to the hills. Now in retrospect the fancy dancing of Van Tuyle and Banks can be seen for the brilliant financial strategy that it was—that not only saved Beverly's neck but the necks of many other health care stocks as well. High-finance techniques—circular financing, stock swaps, rapid capital injections—had been brought to bear on the health care market, and they worked.

Over the next few years many other companies in the health care field tried to mimic the financial maneuvers of Wall Street. Beverly went on to solidify its leadership role by forming a relationship with Hospital Corporation of America: that company surrendered its own nursing homes in exchange for shares in Beverly, so that by early 1983 it owned a fifth of Beverly stock. Elsewhere the owners of two or three hospitals or nursing homes went public in the hope of repeating Frist's success or of being bought out by a larger corporation. More often than not such small companies were gobbled up by Hospital Corporation of America, Humana, National Medical Enterprises, American Medical International, or Beverly, as the giants raced to get ahead of each other.

Attracted by the lucrative investment opportunities in the late 1970s, companies such as Dow Chemical, Monsanto, and Standard Oil were either buying shares in the newly formed health provider firms or themselves setting up health provider divisions. This development had tremendous significance for

11

the industrialization of the health care system. These conglomerates were among the giants of corporate America and they
controlled huge reserves of cash. Their presence in the corporate health care field assured all concerned that the field was
here to stay. A few bad years in a row could have wiped out
even the likes of Hospital Corporation of America, but it would
take a new Ice Age to break Standard Oil or Dow Chemical.
Furthermore, since many of these conglomerates were previously medical suppliers, gone forever was the early important
distinction between medical suppliers and medical providers.
Their presence in the field also hinted at some ominous future
moves; it is virtually assured that today's leaders, such as
Humana or National Medical Enterprises, will one day themselves eventually be acquired by the giants. If the pinch from
new Medicare-Medicaid legislation, such as the new payment
regulations that went into effect October 1, 1983, becomes too
tight, the acquisitions may come sooner rather than later. The
presence of officers from these conglomerates on the boards of
the new companies is surely a sign of things (and more things)
to come.

The health care saga continues with the arrival in 1979 of a
company called ARA Services which bought Spectrum Emergency Care, a large group of emergency care physicians. Here
was a listed corporation, which until then had come no closer to
health care than purveying the food in a number of hospital
cafeterias, buying out a medical group! Not to be outdone by
ARA, Humana also soon purchased its own medical group,
Emergency Medical Services. Corporate America was now in
the business of acquiring medical groups as well as hospitals
and nursing homes.

Several other trends have emerged in the 1980s. The leading
proprietary hospital and nursing home chains grew dramati-
cally; medical suppliers and giant conglomerates solidified
their ownership positions in health provider companies; a

deluge of new health care companies engulfed the stock markets of the country; and corporate provider attention turned toward outside-the-hospital or "free-standing" medical centers (health care facilities not associated with a hospital, set up to provide outpatient services only) as the next frontier. In these years approximately eighty-five new health care listings found their way on to the New York, American, and over-the-counter markets. Investors simply could not get enough action to satisfy their appetites. Three of the most successful of the new medical public offerings were Genentech, Cetus, and American Surgery Centers.

Founded in 1976, Genentech of South San Francisco was taken public by its founders, Swanson, Boyer, and Perkins, in October 1980. The Wall Street reception was incredibly enthusiastic. In March 1981 Dr. Ronald Cape and Dr. P.J. Farley took Cetus Corporation public. Cape, a Princeton biochemist, was an early active supporter of the concept of a genetic engineering industry. For years he stalked the halls of Academe and industry in an effort to start things going. Cape was a good ten years ahead of his time, and though the viability of the industry has yet to be demonstrated, he has helped lay a significant foundation for it.

About a decade earlier two farsighted Phoenix doctors had built the country's first free-standing outpatient surgery center (an independent facility designed for same-day minor operations) near a Phoenix hospital. During the next few years these two, in concert with a number of colleagues, had three other centers built. As interest grew, one of the physicians, John L. Ford, and a financial consultant, Lynn Ray Singley, formed Ford Surgical Centers, a company that provided consulting services for physicians interested in opening their own centers. In 1980 the name of that company was changed to American Surgery Centers, and the business of the company became the building and operation of its own facilities rather than consulting for others. In order to raise capital, the company went public a full two years before its first center was opened in Indianapolis, Indiana, in April 1982. Since then it has opened other centers in Little Rock, St. Louis, Louisville, and Baton Rouge. On the stock market the company saw the value of its shares rise from $0.87 to $18.00 between 1980 and early 1983. Interestingly enough, as of this writing the company has yet to show a single penny profit.

The successful financial experiences of Genentech, Cetus, and American Surgery Centers were to be repeated during these years by many other health care concerns going public for their funding. Investors retain a notable proclivity for health care listings, and the trend continues to accelerate. American Diagnostics, American Electromedics, and American Medi-Dent are but a few more examples of the issues now soliciting and competing for public support.

As for the future, October 1, 1983, may well prove to be another important milestone in the industrialization process. That was the date for the implementation of new legislation pertaining to Medicare-Medicaid payments—sections of the Tax Equity and Fiscal Responsibility Act and new amendments to the Social Security Act. Touted as last ditch efforts to save the Medicare-Medicaid system from bankruptcy, the new regulations provide for prospective payments—that is, they base the amount of money they are willing to pay on diagnosis alone—no matter how many procedures are actually done. Money reimbursed a hospital for an appendix operation, for example, will now be a flat fee, no matter how many X-rays are taken or blood tests are done. This method of reimbursement to profit-seeking corporate hospitals replaces the previous cost plus and service fee, in which payments were made for each procedure, each X-ray, and every blood test plus a percentage of the total billing added on for return on equity (in order to encourage the building of hospitals in the 1960s, the government attracted venture capital by assuring investors a certain return on their money). Naturally, since the profit resulting was a percentage of the total billing, the higher the billing, the higher the profit. Such a system clearly encouraged the use of unnecessary procedures and tests.

There is no doubt that under the new method of reimbursement the hospital chains will have to alter their manner of doing business, but whether the overall impact of the new system will be positive or negative remains to be seen. My feeling is that the listed chains will see their profit margins narrow. The effect of this, however, may be to spur them on to more aggressive acquisition programs.

Given that something like five hundred listed corporations are presently involved in the fierce competition for health care investment dollars, it is amazing to realize that it was only a handful of visionary entrepreneurs who made the decisions that in twenty short years have made health care the largest industry in the country.

The industry, moreover, was recently on the verge of receiving a further badge of legitimacy. In summer 1983, Massachussetts General Hospital, a Harvard Medical School affiliate and one of the most prestigious hospitals in the country, began seriously negotiating the sale of its equally prestigious sister facility, McLean Psychiatric Hospital, to Hospital Corporation of America, in order to finance a needed renovation program at McLean. "In no way," said the Mass. General attorney negotiating the deal, "is this a move on HCA's part to make a fast buck out of McLean. This is a prestige move for them." But after three months of suspense during which the polemics for and against the sale became heated (an editorial opposed to the sale appeared in the *Boston Globe*), the deal finally fell through when Harvard Medical School accepted the recommendation of the McLean staff and deans advisory committee that corporate ownership of their hospital was incompatible with the standards Harvard sets for itself.

It is of further interest to note that one of the people in favor of the sale was George Putnam, the treasurer of Harvard University. Mr. Putnam also happens to be a senior officer of the Putnam Fund, an umbrella investment organization whose subsidiary, Putnam Health Science, held 378,333 shares of HCA as of August 1983. Mr. Putnam has subsequently resigned from Harvard.

In a similar bid for prestige and legitimacy, American Medical International (AMI), the number-two chain hospital owner since its takeover of Lifemark, has in recent months been negotiating for the lease or purchase of the Hospital Center of George Washington University in Washington, D.C., the very hospital where Ronald Reagan was taken after the assassination attempt in spring 1982.

# 3
# PRESCRIPTION FOR PROFIT

I saw Holiday Inn, Kroger, and the A&P; I saw everything
joining together to save expenses.

—THOMAS FRIST, SR.
Founder, Hospital Corporation of
America (1983)

Over the last twenty years the two dominating features of the
American health care system have been the staggering rise in
costs and the tremendously increased involvement of Wall
Street–listed corporations providing primary services and
health care. This year, Americans will spend 10 percent of the
gross national product on health care. The expenditure is more
than double the national defense budget and does not include
the billions more that consumers will spend in order to get fit,
stay slim, eat right, and look well. When the costs of fitness,
diet, and cosmetics are included, the total health care expenditure easily *triples* that for defense. And of every health dollar
spent, an astonishing $0.33—or one-third the total—ends up
in the coffers of listed U.S. firms.

The health care services market collected gross revenues of

$278 billion in 1981 and $317 billion in 1982. Of this money, about 40 percent is spent on hospitalization or for services rendered within hospitals. The figures are exclusive of money spent on research and construction. In the most populous state, California, the average cost of a one-day stay in a hospital went up 22.4 percent to $689 in the twelve months of 1982. In the same time, the average cost per hospital stay went up 10.3 percent to $4,623. The figures represent two to three times the 1982 National Consumer Price Index increase of 6.7 percent.

But cost inflation is only one of the worries for prospective hospital patients these days. Over the last two decades, as we have noted, a new interest has engaged Wall Street, paralleling in significance the meteoric rise of the nation's medical bill. Various public corporations have been buying strings of hospitals, nursing homes, and large physician groups, thus becoming medical providers—providing direct medical services (doctors, hospital care) in addition to having previously played the role of medical suppliers—supplying drugs and secondary services (linens, equipment, food). More recently even doctor groups themselves have been going public. Transactions such as these are examined by the investment community for their financial import but go barely noticed by the bodies that stand to lose or gain the most by the resulting hierarchical rearrangements, namely the general population and the entire medical profession.

The growing corporate ownership of hospital chains and physician groups is at the heart of what has come to be called the "new" Medical Industrial Complex, or MIC, which designates the ensemble of giant corporations involved in one way or another in the business of dispensing health care. Originally the term MIC was coined to describe the loose but influential alliance of drug companies and medical associations. It was first appropriated for use in the present sense in 1980 by Dr. Arnold S. Relman, editor of the *New England Journal of Medicine,* who is also one of the first writers to call attention to the dangers of the corporate takeover.

The rapid takeover by corporations of the health care field is reflected in the speed with which those corporations have grown. Seven of them appear in *Fortune* magazine's 1982 list of the hundred largest diversified service companies, whereas the year before only five appeared. One of them, Beverly Enterprises, is the second-fastest-growing company on the list. Another one, CIGNA, is now the third largest diversified financial company in the country. As of early 1983 listed corporations already owned approximately ll percent of the nation's 5,900 community hospitals. They also had possession of 66 percent of the nursing homes and chronic care facilities countrywide.

These latest corporate acquisitions represent only the advanced stages of the MIC ascendancy. The steady growth over the years of the MIC, with its large proprietary hospital chains and amalgamated physician groups crossing state lines, has changed forever the way health care is dispensed in this country. In the past, the direct patient-doctor relationship constituted the fundamental element in the health care process, and a large share of the health care dollar was spent essentially for physician and surgeon services. But in recent years a growing proportion of that dollar is being eaten away by ancillary costs—hospital beds, drugs, lab tests, expensive medical equipment, etc. Of $1.00 spent on health, only $0.02 now ends up with the physician. And of the $317 billion spent on health care in 1982, fully $118 billion turned up as corporate revenues for the companies of the MIC—corporations dispensing health care in this country in a manner that in my opinion puts some strain on both the laws of the land and the Hippocratic oath.

The corporations involved in the health care system together represent a multibillion-dollar industry that employs ten million Americans. You can own a piece of any one of them by simply phoning your broker and buying the appropriate stock. The companies fall into six main categories:

**1. Listed corporations that own or manage health care facilities such as hospitals, nursing homes, surgical centers, community psychiatric facilities, sports medicine clinics, and rehabilitation centers.** These companies are the ones that are the most visible to the media and the public and the ones most often discussed when the topic of the corporate involvement in health care arises. Well-known examples include Hospital Corporation of America, National Medical Enterprises, and Beverly Enterprises. They have been the subject of feature articles in many newspapers and magazines and have performed consistently well on the New York Stock Exchange. Lesser-known examples include American Surgery Centers and Community Psychiatric, which are listed in the over-the-counter market. Most of these companies have performed spectacularly well for their investors, some having realized gains of up to 600 percent in the course of one year.

With their hospitals (or nursing homes) situated mostly in affluent suburban areas of the country, these companies follow closely similar modes of operation. They buy or build a hospital at a location that they have researched for profitability. At the same time they try to attract a large number of physicians to the area (the more physicians, the more hospitalizations). They then proceed to operate the facility in conformity with bottom-line procedures. These companies have already succeeded in stringing together large numbers of individual facilities, achieving efficiency through the centralization of administration and the mass purchase of equipment and supplies. For the most part the resulting corporate "product" is a clean, efficient, technologically up-to-date facility located more likely than not in a tree-lined suburban area in the West or the Sun Belt. The facility attempts to confine its welcome to insured patients with uncomplicated illnesses. In effect, the parent organizations look upon every bed they own as a profit center.

**2. Listed corporations that have purchased, bought out, or otherwise acquired large medical partnerships.** The activities of these companies belong to probably the least known and least understood aspect of the big business involvement in medicine; they may also turn out to be the most controversial. Essentially such companies have "bought" physicians. The effect, of course, is that profits from the practice of medicine end up in the pockets of company shareholders. Whether this pattern constitutes an instance of illegal professional fee splitting is a matter that will almost certainly one day have to be settled in the courts. Laws in many states, often dating back to the beginning of the century, established rules for professional practices—i.e., medicine, law, etc.—and from the start they deemed intermediate profiteering (that is, any second party profiting on a percentage basis from the practice of medicine and fee splitting) illegal. Examples of such corporations are ARA Services and Humana, both New York Stock Exchange companies. As already mentioned, ARA now owns Spectrum Emergency Care and Humana now owns Emergency Medical Services. The major significance of these acquisitions lies in the consequent for-profit ownership not only of medical facilities but of professional medical personnel as well.

**3. Listed corporations whose primary business is supplying goods and services to the health care field.** Examples are Eli Lilly, Johnson & Johnson, and Baxter Travenol. Many of these companies have long been well-known medical suppliers. The pharmaceutical industry alone took in revenues of $75 billion in 1980 and is expected to take in an estimated $150 billion in 1990. In recent years these suppliers have begun to take on the role of providers as well. Thus Upjohn recently joined with Beverly Enterprises in a project to set up a service company to provide care for the elderly at home. In another example, the president of Hospital Corporation of America also sits on the board of directors of Johnson & Johnson. The industrialization of the health care system has thus allowed the suppliers to now own a piece of the provider action. And the suppliers now have a strong say, an *interested* say, in determining the utilization of the products they produce. The ethical and moral questions presented by such arrangement should be enough to fill a nation of prospective patients with considerable concern.

**4. Listed corporations whose primary business is elsewhere but which, over the last twenty years, have established subsidiaries in the health care field.** Examples include such giants as Du Pont, Dow Chemical, and also ARA Services. Du Pont began a pharmaceutical division in 1966 that in 1982 generated sales of $100 million as part of total revenues of $33 billion for the parent company. Dow Chemical expects the profits from its drug business to increase from $23 million in 1982 to $185 million by 1987. Monsanto Company formed a health care division in January 1983 and has been buying stock in various biotechnology companies.

The companies in this category are considered significant players in the medical-industrial sweepstakes because of the vast capital they have at hand for acquisitional purposes. The blurring of supplier and provider functions that is evident in their investment portfolios presents nothing like the problem that I anticipate in the second stage of the medical industrialization process. For in competition for the enormous potential profits, a "shake-out," or takeover, phase is sure to take place. It is the larger, more successful corporation that will inevitably engulf the smaller as competition grows. These giant corporations will have the strongest hand. One can almost predict that Dow Chemical will one day own National Medical Enterprises—or that a similiar conglomerate will take over a smaller health care corporation.

**5. Listed corporations that supply goods and services to a variety of markets but whose products account for large expenditures by the health care system.** Well-known examples include IBM, Hewlett-Packard, General Electric, and EMI, in addition to the nation's banking and insurance companies. These companies sell high-technology equipment to hospitals and clinics and also provide the financing to facilitate these purchases. They have an inflated importance in the entire scheme because the enormous costs of medical machinery have irrevocably altered the condition of the health care system, making it attractive for corporate involvement. Hewlett-Packard and IBM collect a full 7 percent of their vast revenues from sales to medical markets. Neither company owns hospitals or doctors, but the high cost of their products and the profit potential they represent have interested others in doing so.

**6. Listed corporations that have sprung up in recent years to capture a very specific field in the health care system.** Examples are Cetus and American Surgery Centers. In a sense it was the industrialization of health care that created the climate in which these companies could develop. Their particular concerns include genetic engineering, surgical practices, and psychiatric services—all practiced under individual corporate umbrellas.

The stocks of these companies have performed spectacularly, thus nurturing the view that a health care operation is a good investment. Many of the companies are young and small. It can be anticipated that the more successful among them will eventually be acquired by the corporate giants. The existence of this kind of company proves how easy it is for a health care firm to raise capital on Wall Street; many of them went public with just an idea—even before they had a product to sell.

These then are the six categories of corporations. But as we shall see, they do not operate in isolation. Many are related through common ownership of stock, common board members, and a multiplicity of joint ventures. The approximately five hundred listed corporations involved in health care are frequently webbed together by a network that is almost impossible to unravel but that probably unfairly lowers the investment risks for knowledgeable insiders.

The manner in which you perceive the success of these aggressive corporations clearly varies depending on your socio-political-economic viewpoint. Wall Street investors love these companies because of the spectacular growth they exhibit in size and profit. Indeed one of the difficulties in studying their respective performances is the virtually daily changes in their situations—in subsidiaries acquired, beds owned, and stocks transferred. Almost all the changes have so far meant good news for the investor, and, as a result, the prices of the stocks have been flying high. The price of Beverly Enterprises stock rose from $7.50 to $39.00 between November 1980 and November 1982; American Surgery Centers went from $3.00 to $18.00 in 1983; and Delmed went from $6.00 to $15.00 in the first eight months of 1983. To quote R. Foster Winans in a 1983 *Wall Street Journal* article, "Investor interest in your health care stocks is growing faster than an adolescent's shoe size." In the same article Mr. Winans quotes Jules Marx, a health care analyst with Widlow, Adams & Peck:

> . . . *The index of four smaller home health care issues has risen 94 percent since year-end. Nine nursing home stocks are up an average [of] 41 percent and 11 computer, laboratory, and pharmaceutical stocks show gains averaging 47 percent. These increases compare favorably with a 17 percent rise in the Standard & Poors index of stocks of 500 major U.S. companies.*

The media have also played up the new corporate triumphs because stories about health and money have almost as strong an appeal as stories about sex and violence.

Much of the media output seems to concentrate on the corporate success stories, missing the deeper moral issues. On the other hand, the legitimate medical literature seems to view the subject with academic disinterest or detachment. Conspicuously lacking is an awareness of the nature of the corporate mentality and the workings of the stock market, and of how those features will seriously affect the field. Viewing the moves of corporations in sociological terms, the medical establishment seems to assume an orderly cooperative effort between its profession and the new public investors. In truth, history shows that the corporations simply marched in because there was a profit to be made. Doctors, government, insurance companies, and so-called leaders in health care exercised about as much influence in the situation as a feather in the wind. All they could do was study the phenomenon after the fox had raided the chicken coop.

The companies of the MIC, as we shall see, are interwoven with each other in a complicated maze of ownership and responsibility. They have not yet entered that final competitive phase of corporate life in which, for example, General Motors vies with Chrysler; and IBM with Hewlett-Packard. However, growth by acquisition is the order of the day. Thus Hospital Corporation of America recently acquired both Hospital Affiliates International and Health Care Corporation. And Humana grew tremendously when it "merged" with, or in essence acquired, American Medicorp.

Acquisitions not only signify the economic growth of a company, they also reflect its appetite for diversification. When ARA Services purchased Spectrum Emergency Care, the parent company entered the new field of health provider. Similarly, when Humana purchased Emergency Medical Services, it enabled it to more easily join the fledgling field of the free-standing medical centers. And in August 1983, Extendicare Ltd., a large nursing home operator, formed its own information technology subsidiary, Crowntek Inc., through the acquisition of several small computer firms in the United States and Canada. There is nothing secretive or illicit about these transactions. They are typical of the way in which large corporations grow even larger by gobbling up smaller ones. The acquired companies usually realize substantial profits for their stockholders, and the shares of the acquiring companies often eventually increase in value as well.

Growth by acquisition is no more than good business. My concern, however, is that it may well lead to bad medicine. When a stock is listed on an exchange and is publicly traded, the ultimate ownership of that stock may be difficult to ascertain. An individual or a company may own stock in the individual's or the company's own name, but the stock can also be left in the "street name." The latter arrangement means, for example, that if Merrill Lynch buys a stock for your account, the registered owner of the stock is Merrill Lynch. By and large there are three categories of stock owners: companies, institutions, and individuals. Companies, whether listed or not, may own shares in listed companies. Institutions such as pension funds, mutual funds, and insurance trusts are at present the largest stockholders in the country. Individuals play the smallest role in stock ownership.

The entire public shareholder system is regulated by the Securities and Exchange Commission (SEC), the Federal Trade Commission (FTC), and the Department of Justice. The SEC functions as the internal regulator of the system, assuring that stock trading meets legal requirements. The FTC and the Department of Justice each take a broader view; they keep watch on the interrelationships and the dealings between companies for possible violations of conflict of interest, monopoly (antitrust), or fair-competition laws. Despite such regulations, the general belief is that the system overall is very poorly policed.

In actual practice over a period of time, corporate ownership tends to lead to fewer and fewer hands serving on the boards of more and more companies. Two of the largest corporations in the field, Hospital Corporation of America and Beverly Enterprises, not only own a piece of each other—HCA owns 20 percent of BEV—but have common board members as well. Furthermore, as already noted, the chairman of the board and chief executive officer of HCA also sits on the board of directors of Johnson & Johnson. And BEV and Upjohn have together set up a home care company, Unified Home Health Care. The result is a cozy relationship of joint ownerships and common board members among four large firms—two pharmaceutical giants and two substantial owners of acute and chronic hospital beds.

Other examples abound. INA Health Plan Inc. owns or manages health plan systems serving more than 500,000 members in the states of California, Washington, Arizona, Texas, and Florida. At one stage in their growth INA bought out Ross-Loos, a professional medical partnership. In 1982, INA merged with Connecticut General, the insurance giant, to form CIGNA, a mighty conglomerate whose diverse holdings include insurance companies, doctor groups, and hospitals. INA Management Corporation, a subsidiary of INA—and therefore also one of CIGNA—owns significant numbers of shares of Humana, Hospital Corporation of America, National Medical Enterprises, and Beverly Enterprises. Gerald D. Laubach, a director of Connecticut General, also serves as the president of Pfizer Inc., the large pharmaceutical concern. Humana reached its considerable size by acquiring American Medicorp. And in another typical big-stakes deal Petrolane sold its twenty-four Raleigh Hills facilities to American Medical International for $87 million.

One looks in vain for some form of reaction from the various regulating agencies to this beehive of activity. So far all have been silent on the matter of listed corporations acquiring physician partnerships, although some violation of law may be involved in these transfers.

For a while, the Justice Department objected to the acquisition by ARA of a uniform rental company, Means Services Inc., but it soon dropped its reservations. In August 1982 the FTC filed a complaint on competitive grounds when Hospital Corporation of America acquired Hospital Affiliates International and Health Care Corporation but, again, the objections were later dropped. A subsequent General Accounting Office investigation of the takeover found that room costs were immediately increased $50 per day in some of the hospitals of the expanded chain. Similarly, in early 1982 the Justice Department questioned the acquisition by Beverly Enterprises of Mediplex, but once again the matter was not pursued.

In December 1982 the Justice Department formally charged Petrolane with shuttling patients among its Raleigh Hills facilities in order to avoid Medicare payment ceilings. When the amount of money one state was willing to pay for a particular patient ran out, Petrolane merely shifted that patient to a bed in another state and applied for payment there. Justice also alleged that the Raleigh Hills homes failed to meet state health standards. Petrolane somehow managed to avoid prosecution by selling the facilities. As of this writing, Healthdyne, Inc., of Georgia, intends to acquire 71,000 shares of Narco Scientific. The FTC is investigating the matter for possible antitrust law violation, but, to judge by past example, it is unlikely that the inquiry will result in anything.

There are dozens of other examples that can be cited of listed health care companies forming dubious alliances for purposes of growth and profit, with the regulatory agencies demonstrating only token intervention. As large corporations become more and more involved in medicine, the health care field takes on the appearance of the rest of corporate America, with its fuzzy interrelationships and often explosive acquisitional activity. After all, if Pillsbury can own Burger King and Kellogg can own Mrs. Smith's Pie Company, why can't Hospital Corporation of America own Beverly Enterprises? From the point of view of the corporate system, there is no problem to this arrangement. But many people will rightly want to know who owns the hospital and doctor they have entrusted with their lives.

It is of interest to note that in January 1983 the FTC released a study, labeled Washington Memo 1/7, that focuses on free-standing primary care centers, ambulatory surgery centers, and retail dentistry offices. The report states that the growth of these facilities indicates the large trend toward the commercialization of health care delivery systems as the new corporate providers adopt conventional business strategies in order to maximize profits and finance future expansion. The report goes on to question the quality of care being administered in these facilities. Although its criticisms on the whole are benignly expressed, the document is significant in that it represents the first time government has questioned the quality of corporate medicine.

There is no question, however, that the MIC grew powerful because of the weakness and need that existed in the organizations it overtook. A healthy body politic would not have succumbed so quickly.

Over the last thirty years the health care system had indeed become a haphazard unaffordable compendium of ivory-tower university hospitals; decaying Veterans Administration, state, and county facilities; mismanaged private and religious order hospitals and nursing homes; and tax-exempt wasteful "non-profit" community hospitals. The entire system was held together by a plethora of unintelligible government regulations and programs, private insurance company dictates, and the

29

practices of a medical profession primarily concerned in many instances merely with preserving its own prerogatives in the field. All attempts at reasonable controls were crushed under the cascade of escalating costs. Insurance companies kept raising their premiums; government programs and community hospitals were going broke; and the average citizen was left holding the bag.

It was against this background that the companies that would later become the major hospital chain corporations took a close look at the Medicare and Medicaid legislation of the 1960s and the precarious financial situation of many hospitals, and determined that, using corporate efficiency, discipline, and know-how, they could develop a hospital management system that would deliver quality health care and earn a profit as well. They believed that only the profit motive could reduce soaring costs; and that size in the form of extended hospital or nursing home chains could result in cost saving through centralized administration, common architectural planning, mass purchase of supplies and equipment, and sharing of expensive medical technology.

The initial hospital purchases made by the corporate entrepreneurs certainly kept open the doors of many hospitals that otherwise would have closed for lack of funds. In addition they brought clean, modern, and technologically up-to-date facilities to many communities for the first time. Their ability to attract physicians to these facilities led in a small way to a more reasonable distribution of physicians throughout the country.

Corporate executives insist that it was the lack of administrative know-how that brought so many hospitals to their financial knees. Hospitals, they claimed, needed to acquire a hard-nosed bottom-line mentality in order to survive. Disdain for the profit motive in health care was just a blueprint for rationalizing failure.

They maintain that the physicians who practice in their

hospitals do so in accordance with traditional medical imperatives, and that the number and proportion of hospitalizations, lab tests, and X-rays they call for do not significantly differ from the norm. Indeed Hospital Corporation of America points out that in 1981 the average hospital stay in one of its facilities was 6.4 days, while the national average was 7.6. (More data on the patient mix would be needed to make these figures meaningful, however.) The chains further claim that the heavy media advertising of their hospitals and services does not encourage overutilization or unnecessary utilization of their facilities but simply informs people of their availability; they would also claim that such advertising allows patients to "shop around."

Although all their facilities are fully accredited, the corporations make no bones about attempting to compete with Harvard or Stanford. They are, they claim, in the business of running community hospitals, not of winning Nobel Prizes.

The corporate health care providers are of course corporate entities. Their success in running hospitals is directly related to their ability to compete in the capital markets. In order to do so they must be involved in the day-to-day activities of Wall Street—stock offerings, joint ventures, acquisitions, and divestitures. From the corporate point of view the tangled web of company affairs discussed throughout this book is, far from being deplorable, merely a routine aspect of everyday business. The health care suppliers feel that the only significant thing that has changed recently is that listed companies now own hospitals. This ownership, they would claim, affects only the administration of the hospitals' health care delivery, not its ultimate nature. Moreover the purchase of shares in these health provider companies is carried on in the open market and represents nothing unusual according to business ethics.

While it is true that health care costs have continued to escalate during the era of corporate medicine, the companies claim no responsibility for the system as a whole; after all, they run only 11 percent of the community hospitals of the country.

The corporations claim that only *they* have the necessary capital to build and expand the facilities required for the growing population of the elderly. There can be very little argument on this point. It is interesting to note that in June 1983 the Department of Health and Human Services announced as part of a jobs bill a $10 million home health grant and loan program designed to provide home health care services to the elderly, poor, and disabled in areas where these services are unavailable. It is clear that any workable health care system will have to give a large role to the companies of the MIC.

The corporations like to point out that any highly successful venture brings out the critics. Obviously you cannot please all the people all the time, and it is too early in this new era of corporate medicine to pass final judgments. The for-profits ask to be judged on the quality of the care they deliver and the efficiency of the administrative system they have created. They see their ultimate challenge as providing acceptable health care at reasonable prices in an era of a shrinking medical dollar.

The general attitude of the corporations to their health care role is exemplified by a remark made by Robert Van Tuyle, chairman of the board and chief executive officer of Beverly Enterprises, at the company's 1982 annual meeting. When asked by a union official in the audience who was concerned about Hospital Corporation of America's ownership of 20 percent of Beverly, "What's to prevent a patient from being bounced from one of HCA's hospitals to your nursing homes and then to your home health agencies?" Van Tuyle replied, "That would be a very lucky patient."

In essence, the MIC corporations believe that patients are better off since the corporations have been in the health care business. "We recognize the importance of medical excellence and continue to make it our first priority," the 1982 Humana annual report declares. William A. Fickling, Jr., president and chief executive officer of Charter Medical, states in the company's 1981 annual report, "Providing the best possible patient care always has been one of Charter Medical's major corporate objectives."

The MIC believes that corporate ownership of health care facilities is a nonissue. The same magnificent democracy, they would claim, that allows me to write this book also makes Wall Street health care possible. They argue as well that the system will surely fail in the free marketplace if it doesn't "deliver" as expected. They feel they operate facilities as well as, if not better than, anyone has in the past and they want to be judged on that basis alone. A facility, they claim, should be judged by performance, not by motives.

I fear, however, that in the medicine business, the motive and the performance are so closely related that they amount to the same thing, with consequences that every prospective patient—and that is every one of us—should view with alarm.

# 4
# COUNTRY DOCTOR IN THE BOARDROOM

Were HCA to encounter difficulties in ten or fifteen or more years, HCA executives would have as their first obligation the interests of stockholders rather than the institution of the hospital itself. . . .

—Editorial in the *Boston Globe* (1983)

Years ago a young man or woman who aspired to the calling of medicine went to medical school, earned a degree, put in a year of internship, and then set up a professional office. For those who chose to specialize in a particular branch of medicine— e.g., neurosurgery or gynecology—an additional four or five years of residency was required prior to practicing.

The entire procedure, though demanding, was fairly straightforward: you opened an office and built up a practice. The young doctor then went to the local hospital, presented credentials, and obtained admitting privileges to the hospital. Chances were the hospital was owned by the state, county, or municipality, or by a university or religious order, or perhaps a nonprofit corporation or endowment fund. Until twenty years ago very few private profit-seeking hospital chains existed anywhere, although individual corporate facilities, usually physician owned, do date back fifty years.

The young physician was basically independent. He or she could use whatever laboratory facilities he or she chose and refer patients to whomever he or she preferred. In private practice, the modality of a one-to-one relationship prevailed; the physician examined the patient, prescribed treatment, and then sent the patient the bill. Most of the laboratory tests and X-rays that had to be performed were carried out right in the office.

Naturally the system worked best for those who could afford the services. The poor and disadvantaged, for their part, were expected to seek medical care in state and county facilities. But in the 1950s and 1960s an effort was made to equalize the system. Federal and state governments entered the health care field with a myriad of programs, subsidies, and regulations. Government soon became a substantial third-party payer for health care delivered to the poor and elderly. As of early 1983 federal programs covered forty-three million Americans—twenty-three million on Medicare and twenty million on Medicaid.

He who pays the fiddler calls the tune. With the new programs came an avalanche of requirements to be met and paperwork to be done. Also during these booming years more and more Americans came to be employed by large corporations, which offered various health insurance plans to their personnel—Blue Cross or the like. Life had gotten much more complicated for the solo practitioner. Instead of sending a simple bill directly to the patient he or she now sent it on to a government agency or a private insurance company, and each third-party payer had a different claim form for the physician to fill out. Furthermore a third party was now privy to the patient's medical history, a new situation not without its moral and social implications.

With the tremendous increase in ancillary work, a fourth party now entered, the medical management company, which for a fee kept the doctor's books and did the doctor's billing. So now the medical encounter took place between the physician and the patient, while the financial encounter occurred between the medical manager and the third-party payer. The handling by the medical manager of the myriad necessary bureaucratic forms to be processed transformed the doctor's office into a miniature corporate concern.

By 1982 the average medical office had to deal with eight different means of payment:

| | |
|---|---|
| commercial health insurance plans | 21% |
| Blue Shield | 20% |
| fees paid directly by patients | 20% |
| Medicare | 17% |
| state-subsidized programs | 9% |
| Medicaid | 8% |
| prepaid plans | 3% |
| other sources | 2% |

It is to be noted that only 20 percent of payments now comes from the patients themselves; twenty-five years ago that figure was 80 percent.

Meanwhile, government regulations—in particular the specifics of reimbursement through federal and state entitlement programs—continued to increase. The cost of running a solo practice was becoming prohibitive. Physicians then began banding together in groups—three, four, or more doctors sharing space and facilities. Whereas previously there used to be one cardiologist to an office, there now might be as many as five, all utilizing the same equipment and the same medical and office personnel. And as practices grew so did the necessity for physicians to engage the services of an office manager or medical manager. Now multispecialty groups began to form, running their practice out of free-standing clinics—literally one-stop medical marts offering the whole gamut of medical services. In these facilities each doctor practiced his or her specialization, and at the end of the month he or she received the appropriate remuneration from the office manager.

By the late 1970s it was statistically much more likely for a young physician to join an already established medical group than to start a solo practice. And even though most groups of this sort reimbursed their members with a biweekly or monthly salary keyed to services actually rendered, the overall effect was to make the physician feel like an employee of the group. Coupled with a glut in some specialties, the new arrangement also served to reduce the incomes of many physicians, but at the same time it did reward them with a more predictably scheduled life-style. The solo practitioner was on call every night; the group physician might be on call one night in six.

If doctors' offices began to assume the character of a small business, hospitals began to assume the character of a large one. Hospital ownership in this country is a complicated affair. They can be owned by universities, medical schools, the federal Veterans Administration, or by any other state, county, city, or municipal agency. Hospitals can also be owned by doctors themselves, health plans, religious orders, nonprofit endowment funds, or by public or private corporations. In some cases, a university medical center attached to a private medical school may be owned by the state. Furthermore, any type of hospital may be affiliated with any other convenient institution. By and large, smaller hospitals located in the suburbs and owned privately or by a religious order or health plan are referred to as community hospitals. Some community hospitals are also university affiliated.

Some hospitals are singly owned, while others form part of a larger hospital chain. Chains of hospitals may be owned by corporations, by religious orders, or by health plans such as Kaiser-Permanente.

Every hospital, no matter what its ownership, is essentially a "for-profit" hospital, although many have a tax-exempt status. Every hospital would like to take in more revenues from patients than it spends on them even if it is a state or federal facility. Two primary factors determine which hospitals are fortunate enough to end up in the black at the end of the year. One is the location of the hospital; for location, more than any other variable, decides whether the hospital's typical patient will be sufficiently insured to be able to pay all the bills. The other has to do with how any excess money earned by the hospital is used. A lucky university hospital that finds itself with a year-end surplus will probably reinvest that surplus for teaching and research. Also many religious and nonprofit hospitals pump the extra money back into the plant. If they do not, they may lose their nonprofit status. Privately run doctors hospitals may distribute earnings among the owners, but it is only the corporate chains that earmark a part of net revenues for nonprofessional shareholder profits.

In an effort to improve medical care and capture shifting populations, a hospital building boom occurred in the 1960s and 1970s; but by the late 1970s more hospital beds existed than were necessary in most areas of the country. By 1981, in the country as a whole, 4.4 hospital beds were available per 1,000 population. A subtle competition now began between different institutions in the quest for client/patients. Contesting hospitals purchased every new piece of expensive medical gadgetry that hit the market—sometimes even what was already owned by another hospital only blocks away. One machine, the CT scanner, a million-dollar piece of equipment, initially was found only in large academic medical centers. Within a few years, however, it seemed that every local community hospital had one. In San Mateo County in California, for example, there are six hospitals within a ten-mile radius of each other, and each hospital features a scanner. In the American way, every competing doctor and hospital was expected to own all the latest trappings—computers, scanners, automated test equipment, etc. To further complicate matters, some counties refused to send ambulance patients to facilities that lacked a scanner or heart-bypass machine at the ready twenty-four hours a day. In addition, cardiac surgeons often refused to admit their patients to hospitals that lacked the latest paraphernalia, and neurosurgeons and ophthalmologists insisted on the latest in space-age laser technology as well. It used to take a new piece of medical equipment years to gain acceptance, but now, within a few weeks an experimental machine still fresh from the mold is part of the standard equipment of every community facility. The wizards of Silicon Valley always had a great deal to sell to the medical profession, and the price was always high. But in order to compete, hospitals and physicians felt they had to buy, and eventually the bills came due. A new set of problems appeared.

With regard to the million-dollar CT scanner, for example, the rule of thumb had been that the machine would pay for itself in two years in a five-hundred-bed hospital with an emergency room seeing twenty-five thousand cases per year. That calculation assumed, however, that the next scanner was stationed at least a few miles away, so that sufficient patients would be available. By 1980, however, that condition no longer prevailed. In fact some two-hundred-bed hospitals now owned a scanner and many of them did not even have an emergency room. In short, for many, many hospitals the patient load was insufficient to support the proliferation of expensive and not always necessary equipment.

As operating and financing and billing became ever more complicated, hospitals found themselves hiring more and more professional hospital administrators, so that by the late 1970s hospital medical staffs had almost entirely ceded control to the new army of trained bureaucrats. Doctors, as a consequence, began to feel more and more like employees, with their autonomy curtailed by the hierarchical rigidity of the new system.

Even as physicians were experiencing harder times, so were hospitals beginning to feel a different kind of squeeze. More and more people came to be covered by government programs such as Medicare or various state programs (not all of them "cost-plus") which, because of astronomically rising costs, incompletely covered the hospital's expenses. (A cost-plus option, in which billing is made for all expenses incurred plus a guaranteed profit, would, of course, have assured hospital solvency but would perhaps program bankruptcy as well.)

To understand the implications of this shortfall, think of a hospital as a very expensive hotel, $500 per night, with very high overhead costs. In 1981 in California, for example, 28 percent of hospital patients were supported by either Medicare or MediCal (the California state plan) or some combination of the two. Think how long a Sheraton or a Hilton hotel could stay in business if 28 percent of its guests omitted paying a portion of their bill. And although hospitals were already collecting less than they needed to remain financially afloat, in 1982 there occurred a further 37 percent increase in the discrepancy between the amount the nation's hospitals billed various government programs and the amount the programs reimbursed them.

In the new circumstances, university hospitals were able to manage, though with growing difficulty, because of support from the medical school and the university itself. Religious-order hospitals, especially the Catholic hospitals, also managed more or less. State and county facilities experienced a very rough time, and throughout the country many were forced to close their doors. The community and isolated proprietary hospitals had a difficult time as well. Under the pressure some

41

of them attempted to pool resources and to form loose associations, but eventually many either closed or tried to sell. And of those hospitals that chose to sell, many found eager buyers among the corporations of the MIC.

By far the most significant change in health care delivery of the 1970s, and its greatest disappointment, was the concept of prepaid medicine provided by a health maintenance organization or HMO. Initially trumpeted as the surest means to deal with escalating health costs, and a cause of great excitement in the entire health care field, most HMOs failed miserably in those years through mismanagement, greed, and lack of capital to stay the course.

In prepaid medicine, a subscriber pays a fixed amount per year in advance to the HMO and then receives all medical care in the organization's facilities without further payments. Kaiser-Permanente is the most successful operation of its kind, owning even its own hospitals. The system is supposed to save money because the insurer and the provider are one and the same, and thus a vested interest in preventing illness and avoiding unnecessary tests and hospitalizations naturally exists. Certainly if a subscriber pays Kaiser $500 in advance and then no more, it is to Kaiser's benefit to keep that patient healthy and out of the hospital.

HMOs in the modern sense first began operating in 1929. They never really caught on, except for Kaiser, until after President Nixon signed the Health Maintenance Organization Act of 1973, which made available federal grants and loans to stimulate their formation. The legislation also stipulated that employers of at least twenty-five workers must make available to employees the opportunity to join an HMO if one existed in the area.

The HMO concept, with variations here and there, became the rage in the late 1970s, until one by one, with very few exceptions, they went broke. The general plan was to set up a pre-negotiated fee schedule with participating physicians and hospitals, and then sign up subscribers who would prepay for premium medical coverage. The problem was that, unlike Kaiser physicians, the participating physicians in most other HMOs practiced out of their own offices or hospitals, and the HMO patients constituted only a small part of their practice. These physicians had no vested interest in keeping costs down; again unlike Kaiser physicians, they did not share in any end-of-year profits. Thus as soon as the federal matching funds available to set them up ran out, most HMOs went belly up. President Reagan for his part subsequently halted any new grants to HMOs; and private investors and corporate entities began to move in to supply the new money.

Given the prevailing tough times for both hospitals and physicians, you might well wonder at the eagerness of the buyers. For one thing, in the 1970s, prospective buyers finally concluded that a universal Medicare program was not about to be passed into law. Before this time almost everyone involved in the medical and hospital professions, especially the American Medical Association, lived with the fear that one day the United States government would institute a federal- or state-run health program, like those in Great Britain and Canada. Senator Edward Kennedy's continued efforts to put together such a program had always sent chills through large sections of the medical community. But by the late 1970s most observers agreed that the government could not afford, either politically or economically, to undertake such a vast and expensive program.

Even before this time some interested corporations had already taken a hard look at Medicare and Medicaid legislation and decided that it had a profit potential. They concluded that given an efficient high-volume operation the payment schedules under the two plans were more than generous and would allow for a healthy profit to be made. For example the legislation moved for a built-in profit (or a so-called return on equity capital) for proprietary hospitals, over and above the payments made to nonprofit hospitals, in order to entice private investors to the field. By the 1980s the guaranteed profit margins had reached the order of 19–20 percent. In October 1983 federal investigator Richard P. Kusserow questioned not only what he considered to be the excessive amount of profit but also the legality of applying the return-on-equity criterion to home health care systems, where no physical plant calling for large capital investment is involved. Indeed, when Congress passed the Medicare Act in 1965, providing government-subsidized care, federal officials estimated that the costs of the plan might reach $8.8 billion by 1990. But Medicare costs had already surpassed that figure in 1972, and by 1981 the costs had risen to $42.5 billion. For fiscal 1983 Medicare spent $60 billion, a seventeen-fold increase since 1967—it was not enough to keep some smaller hospitals afloat!

Not only, then, were the Medicare and Medicaid payment schedules reckoned by some corporate planners to be relatively ample for their purposes, but these same planners also correctly surmised that once begun the new programs would be politically impossible to abandon or cut back. Essentially Medicare (or Medicaid) agrees to pay 80 percent of reasonable patient costs; the arrangement clearly favors a high-volume cost-cutting manner of operation. The system inadvertently rewards waste and overutilization, thereby fostering its own rising cost. The corporate planners also looked at the census figures and found them auspicious for their purposes too. For in the 1970s the average age of America's population was climbing, and the trend meant a certain increase in health care utilization. Whereas in 1980 the big population bulge occurred among those in their thirties, by the year 2000 the bulge will occur among those in their forties, a time when many bodies begin to show some wear and tear. Furthermore between 1970 and 1980 the group of the population age sixty-five years and older increased by 65 percent; the age group eighty-five plus increased by 60 percent. By the year 2000 the number of those sixty-five and older will increase another 28 percent to equal twenty-seven million people.

Statistics show that for every doctor's visit and hospitalization for a twenty-year-old, there are three for a thirty-year-old, five for a forty-year-old, eleven for a fifty-year-old, and twenty-six for a sixty-year-old; both the need and the investment opportunities grow with age. It is of some interest that in 1981 8 percent of the Medicare population accounted for 66 percent of Medicare costs, and that 28 percent of that amount was spent during the last year of the patient's life.

Coupled with the anticipated increase in acute care needs will be a similar increase in chronic and nursing care needs. As the population gets older so will the elderly, gaining in numbers, in political power, and so will their demands intensify for more attentive care. At present there is an extreme shortage of chronic care and skilled nursing facilities for the elderly. It is estimated that by 1990 the country will need 250,000 more nursing home beds than exist now. Whatever their ulterior motives, one should credit the corporations for being the first to turn public attention to this special health care need.

As for HMOs, although the early ones failed, they nevertheless helped spawn the general idea of pre-negotiated fee schedules of special interest to the MIC. For example, recent changes in the applicable laws in the state of California now allow the state to pre-negotiate fee schedules for MediCal patients with contracting hospitals. More significantly the new laws also allow for private carriers such as Blue Cross to pre-negotiate fee schedules for their subscribers. Private health insurance carriers depend for their success to a great degree on group contracts signed with large companies, and the new laws

45

facilitate such arrangements. One listed insurance company can now provide lucrative health insurance for the employees of another listed company, and the whole deal can be pre-negotiated with a medical provider that is also a listed company. Furthermore the three companies involved may be inter-related or even subsidiaries of the same giant corporation. The premiums end up cheaper, but in the absence of any significant physician control, so also might the care.

The advent of the prepaid medical plan suited the designs of the corporations. In the contest for large prepaid contracts involving substantial numbers of subscribers, the corporation can underbid anyone. Corporations can also absorb a loss and tolerate loss leaders. Furthermore with prepaid subscribers a large amount of "up-front" cash is usually a part of the transaction, an attractive bonus for the contractor; the money is in the till before the services are delivered.

The HMO debacle played into corporate hands in yet another fashion. Here was another system in which the physicians were essentially employees.

Corporations can succeed where everyone else has failed because of their financial resources. And unlike the failing HMOs, they can count on added profits from the ancillary services they offer. When an insurance company buys out an HMO it can take the up-front subscriber money and invest it at much higher returns than anyone else because of its high-volume business. And no corporation minds losing a million dollars in an HMO when it's making $2 million in increased related services. In short, the corporations could not care less about what system they buy because in the end it is only the profits that count. The HMO happens to constitute a particularly attractive package for MIC interests because it is by its nature a business enterprise. As a business enterprise it can be bought. Blue Cross already owns some "take care" HMOs and, all things considered, Kaiser-Permanente seems to be a sitting duck for a buy-out.

The corporations now taking over will not make the mistakes that the early HMOs made. They will make sure they own their own hospitals and their own physicians, and they will also possess sufficient capital to make success certain. The delivery of quality care is another matter. Medical care, unlike food, is not an easily itemizable commodity. Every day things are done in a doctor's office or a hospital that do not make economic sense but are in the best interests of the patient.

Kaiser works as well as it does and is as admirable as it is because its physicians have at least a small say in the running of the company, and when economics have to be sacrificed to quality care, then so be it. Nobody expects physicians to be in charge when Humana and National Medical Enterprises set up their HMOs; nor were they given much of a say when insurance giants such as Connecticut General were making decisions.

HMOs are neat affairs, and it's to be expected that more and more of them will be scooped up by the MIC as they run out of money. When that happens physician control over the quality of the health care delivery will diminish even further.

The MIC is betting that Americans will be willing to sacrifice quality for economy. Its position has been formulated on the basis of results taken from surveys, census reports, and questionnaires circulated in communities across the country. What the corporations do not understand, in my opinion, is that Americans, and in particular their elected officials, are notorious for the habit of seeking ways to cut medical costs for their next-door neighbors; but for themselves and their families they expect the very best. The contradiction is natural and normal, and we are a long way off from deliberately sacrificing quality for economics where our own families are concerned. But it is likely that the end result of the HMO debacle will be to put more hospitals and physicians under corporate control, thus leaving more and more Americans with fewer options in their choice of medical care.

At the present time, variations of HMOs are being tested by both employers and insurers. The most common twist is the cost-incentive mechanism: the employees pay a much lower deductible if they utilize specified cheaper providers. The most recent HMO variation is the preferred provider organization, or PPO. Brought into prominence by the California Blue Cross prudent buyer concept, the PPO pre-negotiates fees with hospitals and physicians to care for its subscribers. In many instances there are few differences other than administrative ones between HMOs and PPOs; but the PPOs are perhaps a little more eager to compete for new groups of clients. Unlike California with its new laws, many states prohibit insurers from influencing subscribers' choice of provider through financial incentives. Representative Ron Wyden, a Democrat from Oregon, has proposed Bill HR 2956—"Preferred Provider Health Care Act"—to override state laws that prevent the formation of PPOs and to provide limited antitrust exemption where it is deemed necessary. Passage of the legislation will have a major impact on health care providers. It will force hospitals to compete in order to be included as a provider on every PPO list. It will also no doubt keep the door open to the financial speculators who rode their HMOs high and low in the 1970s. The new medical shake-out promises to be equally bloody.

By most reckoning, the corporate push into medicine was not so much different from what was happening in many other fields in this country in the late 1960s and 1970s. Mom and Pop stores, cottage industries, family farms, and small businesses found themselves facing off against the juggernaut of investment capital, and coming off second best. Fields such as agriculture, horse-farming, book publishing, and entertainment began to fall at this time, more or less under corporate sway. Do corporations enter a particular field to come to its

rescue? Or when they sense the possibility of a profit? Whatever else can be said on the subject, it is certain that there is
something in the nature of the corporate beast that requires it
to grow in order to remain viable on its own terms. And when
the traditional industries ceased to be acceptable takeover
targets, the corporate embrace turned elsewhere.

Why then did corporate America rush into health care? Why
has it been so successful? The truth is that many corporations
took a hard look at the health care field and decided for fiscal
reasons alone to move in. It is doubtful whether these companies themselves foresaw acquiring such a large chunk of the pie
in so short a time.

When a corporation decides to enter or expand activities
within a field it considers three main factors:

1. the product being sold and the perceived need for the
   product;
2. the prevailing market conditions; and
3. the ease of raising capital for the venture.

The "commodities" the corporations now looked at were
drugs, technology, financing, hospital beds, auxiliary services,
and the professional services themselves. Of these items only
hospital beds and professional services represented new con-
cepts as corporate products; the others had long come within
the compass of the corporate health supplier. Now in order to
succeed as health care providers the corporations needed the
cooperation, conscious or otherwise, of physicians, for hospitals and nursing homes become populated when physicians
consign patients to them. The conquest (by gentle persuasion,
of course) of the medical profession by corporations was therefore a vital step in the operation.

Two major matters facilitated the conquest. In the heavily
and moderately populated areas of the country, a glut of
physicians has occurred, forcing many of them to accept

positions they would have spurned a few years ago. Second, with rising costs and the rising demands of technology and bureaucracy, it has become increasingly difficult to operate an individual medical practice.

In order to attract physicians to its operations, corporations advertise prominently in the various medical journals, promising to relocate prospective joiners in the community of their choice—that is, to help set up the practice, find a family home, enroll the kids in the local school—so long, of course, as the community is close to a corporation hospital. These physicians, however, are then expected to locate their office in a corporation-owned building, use the corporation's labs for medical testing, admit their patients to the corporation hospital, and refer them when necessary to other physicians belonging to the corporation.

In many instances the corporation will also promise to take care of all the bookkeeping associated with the practice—this for a percentage or high fee, which amounts to fee splitting: the corporation is directly profiting from the practice of medicine. Whether the financial arrangements between physicians and corporations are illegal, as I suspect they are, will ultimately be a matter for the courts to decide.

The emergence and subsequent rapid growth of the Medical Industrial Complex really represents the simultaneous convergence of several trends in the health care system. Physicians were losing their taste for the complexities and expenses of solo practice, and hospitals were feeling the tremendous economic pressure brought on by government-subsidized patients and an explosion in costs of sophisticated medical equipment. Everyone "knew" that medical care was too expensive and that doctors were making too much money. The celebrated Medicare and Medicaid mills that specialized in overbilling and phantom billing in high-volume operations aroused public

50

indignation with their often fraudulent practices. And people had the feeling that health care had become a much too impersonal transaction.

Perhaps more careful regulation by government and more voluntary cooperation among hospitals and among doctors might have saved the day, but as it was, in the 1970s in this country, medicine went up for sale. The age of the supermarket mentality in medicine was born.

# 5

# CLOSING THE CIRCLE: PROVIDERS, SUPPLIERS, AND PATIENTS

Health care is not a commodity like a pair of shoes or a used car or a refrigerator.

—ARNOLD S. RELMAN, M.D. editor
*New England Journal of Medicine* (1983)

As I already noted, the low probability of the passage of a universal medical insurance program, the relatively generous Medicare and Medicaid payment schedules for large-scale cost-efficient operations, the financial miseries of many hospitals, the growing employee mentality of many physicians, and the concomitant aging of America aroused the interest of the business speculators. There were other factors as well. Health care after all is a recession-proof "industry"; regardless of the economic climate, people get sick and need care. Here then was an operation that was not seasonal and promised to grow for at least the next forty years. Medicine itself is a high-cash-flow, low-inventory, low-investment affair—all appealing character-istics from the investor viewpoint.

The hospital and health care conglomeration, or, as some writers have called it, "the mediglomeration," is a large and sprawling complex, an industry now accounting, as we've seen, for some 10 percent of the gross national product. The Department of Health and Human Services is the largest bureaucracy in Washington, indeed the largest bureaucracy in the world. No wonder that the corporate planners found the field inviting.

In many ways industry had always been deeply involved in medicine. Private companies manufactured drugs and medical equipment; they built, equipped, and supplied hospitals with everything from food to linens; they sold health insurance; and they leased computers—in short they purveyed just about all the products and services needed by the medical field. Involved as they were, however, industry had stayed outside the command structure of health care; it did not own the hospitals and it did not employ the physicians. But the prospects were too inviting to resist for long. A secure circle is formed when the goods of the supplier (drugs, food, linens, X-rays, etc.) are assured a steady sale by the interested decisions of the provider.

A crucial commonly known fact in medicine is that health care utilization in a particular locality is directly proportional to the number of physicians in the locality. On the whole, four doctors in a community will fill twice as many hospital beds, prescribe twice as many drugs, carry out twice the number of appendectomies, and order twice the number of X-rays and lab tests compared with two doctors in a community. Health care utilization in this sense is dictated by physicians, not patients.

Doctors are indeed the main dispensers of available medical services. They alone have made the tremendous investment in a lengthy education and training process. From the time they leave high school it takes the average specialist twelve years and $210,000 before the first patient is seen—enormous expenditures of time and money by any standard.

And so the corporations, with their pills, linens, and hospital beds, eagerly attempted to entice doctors to "their" areas. The corporations involved would now make a direct profit from the practice of medicine and from the food, drugs, machinery, and medical necessities that accompany hospitalization.

Food, to take that example, is often overlooked when considering the medical dollar. But consider again the analogy of hospital as hotel, where this time all the guests eat every meal in and many guests are on special diets. Spend a week at a decent big-city hotel and order every meal from room service and see what that costs you. Hospital food is an extremely lucrative business, and there are several listed companies doing very well that do nothing else. Remember also that food is only the beginning; there is cutlery, linens, and the myriad other everyday items that human beings require while in confinement.

ARA is one of the companies that supplies food to hospitals; it also supplies linens and various vending machines. As already mentioned, the company recently purchased Spectrum Emergency Care, partly to diversify but also to help fill the beds of hospitals, many of which serve ARA food.

Drugs are another lucrative medical sideline. Although only a licensed physician can prescribe certain controlled substances that go into drugs and medicines, it is estimated that for every prescription filled, one thousand "over-the-counter" remedies are purchased. The pharmaceutical industry is extremely competitive but the profits that accrue to the successful participants are enormous. Listed companies such as Merck, Johnson & Johnson, Ciba, and Abbott are the industry giants. Their salesmen try to maintain contact with every physician in the country, and there is hardly a physician alive who hasn't received a gift or free sample from one of them; many a physician's "black bag" was a pharmaceutical company's gift. These companies already own substantial shares in companies such as ARA, Humana, Hospital Corporation of America, and National Medical Enterprises—firms that own hospitals or physician groups. Whether or not any improprieties actually exist is not easy to determine, but so long as companies that provide health care are publicly held—and held by drug suppliers—the potential for trouble is real.

The pharmaceutical companies always have had a vested interest in physicians overprescribing, and certainly companies such as Humana have a vested interest in overhospitalizing. Now there exists a loose corporate mosaic having a vested interest in the overutilization of all aspects of the health care system. All this costs not only the patient but everyone else, because when a physician prescribes Valium for a patient on Medicare or Medicaid, part of that prescription is underwritten by the federal government. Similarly, for example, if a Humana physician were to hospitalize a Medicare or Medicaid patient needlessly, part of the costs are underwritten by the federal government.

The mediglomeration did not invent overutilization; the practice has been common for the last forty years. In fact the federal government in 1980 estimated that only one Valium prescription in thirty was really medically necessary, and only one hospitalization in eight was medically indicated. Early in 1983 the General Accounting Office produced a memo asserting that many health care services provided to Medicare and Medicaid recipients are medically unnecessary and should not be paid for by the government.

A look at clinical laboratories reveals some insights into the general problem Blood tests began as a very specialized discipline in the mid-nineteenth century and gained acceptance slowly. In the early years the clinical laboratories were located almost exclusively in large teaching hospitals. In 1889 the Johns Hopkins Hospital opened a laboratory under the direction of the pathologist William Welch. In 1896 Richard C. Cabot published *Clinical Examination of the Blood*, one of the first works of its kind in English. Gradually at first and then with a rush, clinical laboratories became an integral (and expensive) part of health care.

Since 1960 the volume of laboratory tests has been increasing by at least 15 percent each year. Tests accounted for an astounding 10 percent of the total health care bill, or $31 billion, in 1982. While part of the high expense can be attributed to the increased sophistication of medicine, many of the tests remain excessive and unnecessary. Many factors, including a profit motive, the poor understanding of some physicians (alas) of the nature of the tests they order, and the growing sway of medical-legal considerations, have produced this regrettable situation.

Whatever the reasons for too many tests, only the physicians themselves can order them, regardless of what kind of hospital employs them. Some medical institutions have recently begun to make a concerted effort to cut down on tests. Some teaching institutions, by means of special seminars, chart reviews, and financial incentives, have begun to train their residents to limit them. And in 1982 the Los Angeles County-USC Medical Center called for a reduction in tests performed in order to deal with cutbacks in federal, state, and county funding. The medical auditors had found that certain thyroid function tests were being ordered too frequently because of physician misconception as to the function of the test. Simply clarifying the order form had the desired effect. However, in the corporate sector there has been little evidence of a similar effort at self-regulation. The profits to be gained are too tempting.

The corporate giants that supply the X-ray machines, CT scanners, computers, and other very expensive sophisticated surgical paraphernalia have a vested interest in the maximum utilization—the unnecessary utilization—of this equipment. None of these giants presently owns a hospital or a physician group, but they do own shares in companies that do. The more physicians there are, the more Hewlett-Packard electrocardiogram machines will be needed; ditto for IBM computers, Picker X-ray machines, and GE CT scanners. The suppliers now own shares in the hospitals that buy the machines from them; they also own shares in the physician groups that prescribe the use of the machinery for their patients. The present freewheeling system leaves open the possibility of unholy alliances. So long as the stocks of medical care providers are traded on the open market, the potential for price-fixing, monopolies, and overutilization exists.

From the corporate point of view owning hospitals and doctors has a nice ring to it. Everyone wants to be a doctor. The new market ethos has made it possible to be a doctor "by proxy"—by buying shares in companies such as ARA or Humana. Merrill Lynch is bullish on doctors!

The corporations knew full well that in entering the hospital field they would be competing against hospitals benefiting from a Sec. 501(c)(3) tax-exempt status. Despite the handicap they felt they could succeed, and they were right. Corporate entities had plenty of capital, as well as the ability to raise it in a hurry—an ability the traditional health care providers always lacked. There the corporations were, standing on the sidelines when so many hospitals were up for sale. They bought. Many nursing homes too went up for sale at this time because their private owners were growing increasingly frustrated by wave after wave of new regulations. Their depreciation schedules had run their course, and their property values had increased substantially. Few were able to resist the offers of the corporations.

Once a corporation gets involved in a venture its shareholders expect growth. If this year the company owns ten hospitals, the next year it will be expected to own twenty. If the company cannot find ten more hospitals to buy, then it will be expected to acquire some corporation that already owns them. The population of America had polarized into inner-city dwellers and suburbanites by the late 1960s. Generally speaking, university, state, and county hospitals served the inner cities. Predictably the corporations ignored the cities and took dead aim at the country's 5,900 suburban community hospitals; the medical profits were in the suburbs, for that is where most of the country's privately insured families live.

As of early 1982 there were 437,688 physicians in the United States, and 200,000 of them were already admitting patients to hospitals owned or managed by one or another of the mediglomerate companies. As already mentioned, 11 percent of community hospitals and 66 percent of all nursing homes are now in the corporate domain. It is projected that by 1990 there will be a 40 percent increase in the number of physicians and, if the present trend continues, an even greater proportion of them than before will be working for the "company."

In a few cases, as we have seen, doctors *are* the company, or they at least started the company. Whether they are employers or employees, however, corporate involvement results in a transformation of their methods and aims and ultimately the care they provide. Eventually, the alchemists who turn science into gold turn themselves into just another marketable product. The transformation of emergency medicine is a case in point. Every American is familiar with the hospital emergency room. In 1982 one out of two Americans visited an emergency room at least once during the year and paid an average bill of $67. In the last fifteen years so-called emergency medicine has become a big business and has operated in a manner more in keeping with corporate requirements than with medical necessity. In fact one could say that emergency room physicians were the first ones to accommodate themselves to the new order in medicine, and they accommodated themselves handsomely.

There presently exist in the country 5,200 full-service, hospital-based and an additional 1,100 free-standing emergency rooms. Fifteen thousand full-time physicians and 45,000

59

additional part-time physicians work in these facilities. Also involved are 60,000 emergency nurses, 450,000 emergency medical technicians, and 32,000 paramedics. Furthermore there are now over 40,000 ambulances and 70 medical helicopters attached to the operation. Countrywide 63 emergency-medicine training programs exist to provide up-to-date instruction for interested physicians. All in all, including secretaries and clerical workers, a cast of over one million health care workers and a budget of over one billion dollars (for supplies and equipment only) serve the system.

It was not always so. Many years ago hospital emergency rooms were routinely staffed by hospital staff physicians on a rotational basis. Physicians were obligated to do this as part of their training or in order to maintain their admitting privileges to the hospital. The emergency room was also a good place to meet the community and build up a practice. You saw a child with a cold and you told the parents to bring the child back to your office in one week for a checkup. You acquired a new patient.

On any given day in an emergency room, you might have been treated by a pediatrician, an internist, a surgeon, or a gynecologist, depending upon who was on call. The doctor who saw you sent you a bill. But beginning in the early 1960s hospitals started having trouble in their emergency rooms. Lawyers began suing when, for example, a surgeon messed up a simple heart case that could easily have been handled by an internist. Similarly, pediatricians started getting into trouble dealing with multiple-trauma cases. The emergence of the drug culture and its attendant medical problems also began to present difficulties to the various specialists unfamiliar with the physical and psychological specifics of the subject. Soon staff physicians began avoiding their shifts in the emergency room.

Concurrently the American Heart Association began insisting on the need for adequate pre-hospital care and CPR (cardio-pulmonary resuscitation) availability—both at the scene of a disaster and in the emergency room. The skills involved were ones that the average staff doctor did not have. Later the American College of Surgery began a similar campaign for better emergency room care for trauma victims. It was then that a number of small groups of physicians around the country began to promote the idea that emergency room medicine should itself be a medical specialty. The specialty moreover promised to be one that would offer an all-around comfortable life for its practitioners. Emergency room doctors would benefit from a steady clientele, the absence of office overhead, and a fixed schedule that allowed for a pleasant lifestyle—i.e., no more phone calls in the middle of the night. Once you finished your shift the chest pains became some other doctor's problem. The money, as in most medical specializations, promised to be excellent.

Initially hospitals welcomed these pioneer physicians, allowing them to practice in the hospital emergency room and to bill the patients directly. For the hospital the new setup proved to be a boon because, among other things, it no longer was faced with the headache of forcing staff physicians to put time in what they considered the "pit." More and more hospitals began seeking out full-time emergency physicians to staff their emergency rooms. By the mid-1960s such physicians were much in demand, and as a result they did very well financially.

The ensemble of full-time emergency room physicians constituted at this time a ragtag group of residency dropouts, ski and surf bums, and retirees. As a group these doctors had the reputation for being not too competent, and consequently their hospital standing was not too high. Things, however, soon changed. Many hospitals soon realized that emergency rooms could comprise an excellent source of revenue, and they sought more control in their management. They began to institute a system of contracting with a single doctor to provide a team of emergency room physicians. In the new arrangement the hospital would bill the patient and remit a fixed percentage of that bill to the contractual physician; that physician would share the revenues with the other doctors of the emergency room staff, who were either his partners in the group or hired by the group on fixed salaries. Thus the physician who worked with an 85 percent "contract" would receive $85,000 a month from the hospital if he or she billed $100,000, minus a sum agreed upon to account for bad debt.

These emergency room contracts suffered from several defects. First, they were in all likelihood illegal, in that the manner of payment constituted overt fee splitting: a physician is forbidden by law to share in any way a percentage of his or her billings. Second, the percentages withheld by the hospitals (technically in order to pay for doing billings) were extravagant. In subsequent years, as hospitals began to be pinched, 85 percent contracts were negotiated down to 60 percent and even 50 percent. The illegality and the hospital extravagance persist today. Moreover, these "contracts" are by and large ninety-day cancellable affairs, so that emergency room physicians serve more or less at the pleasure of the hospital administration.

These physician groups themselves were often mini-corporations. A physician who contracted with one hospital could profit more if he or she contracted with two or three and sometimes (why not?) nine or ten hospitals. In each case the physician would sign a contract with a given hospital and then engage other physicians to do the work.

Suppose Dr. Jones signed an 85 percent contract with St. Joseph Hospital. He subsequently would hire five or six emergency room physicians who would be paid $30 an hour for their work. If that group billed for $100,000 per month the hospital would remit $85,000 to Dr. Jones, who would then pay "his" physicians. The profits for Dr. Jones were substantial, especially if he contracted with many hospitals.

Over time, emergency medical groups evolved into two distinct types. From the first, or nonhierarchic type, large medical partnerships developed in which all physician partners shared in the profits. In the second, or entrepreneurial type, profit sharing was restricted to a few individual partners, while all other physicians engaged by the group received fixed salaries as its employees. An example of the nonhierarchic type is California Emergency Physicians, which holds contracts with thirty-three different hospitals in California; an example of the entrepreneurial type is Spectrum Emergency Care, which contracts with over two hundred facilities across the country. Spectrum's profits used to go to three or four individuals, but after it was acquired by ARA services in 1979, they now are part of ARA consolidated earnings.

While some emergency physicians pursued their wheeler-dealer instincts, others helped organize a professional society that came to be known as the American College of Emergency Physicians (ACEP). The purpose of the society was supposedly to regulate the profession and to enhance the general image of emergency room physicians. The real purpose of the organization was to sell to the public and to the medical establishment as a whole the notion that emergency medicine represented a distinct medical specialty that called for appropriately trained physicians to engage in its practice. ACEP actively asserted its position because many hospitals resisted the contracting process and continued using staff physicians in the emergency room.

Eventually, in 1979, the organization succeeded in its aim: emergency medicine was recognized as the twenty-third medical specialty by the American Board of Medical Specialties. The decision had the effect of subjecting hospitals to tremendous pressure from legal and government sources to engage bona fide emergency physicians for their facilities. County officials began insisting that hospital emergency rooms must be specially staffed in order to become base stations for the increasing number of paramedic mobile units. Naturally the cost of emergency medical care rose under the new system. It is interesting to note, however, that many nonemergency doctors still believe the whole concept of an emergency medical specialty is erroneous: emergency medicine is no more than available medicine; staff doctors could easily be trained to be competent emergency room personnel.

Inevitably, however, the existing large emergency groups competed hotly for the newly available contracts, and many of them grew even larger. By the mid-1970s emergency room medicine was unlike any other medical field: it was big business pure and simple. The medical megagroup had come of age—which certainly facilitated corporate takeovers later on. In 1980 the total emergency room bill for the country came to $10 billion, of which about half went to physicians and half to hospitals. It is the extraordinary sums and profits involved that made emergency room medicine an obvious target for the MIC.

But by operating as entrepreneurs, emergency physicians also planted the seeds of their own destruction. Whereas a few of them profited handsomely early on by selling their relatively small practices to a corporation, most suffered dearly when hospitals succeeded in steadily renegotiating contracts down, each time taking a bigger and bigger slice of the pie. The hospitals always cited financial hardship as a reason, but in reality they were just playing the entrepreneurial game as well. In 1975 the average emergency room contract in California had a physicians' split of 72 percent, but by 1980 that split was down to 66 percent. The early big money drew many doctors to the field, and now there is a glut of them—which is just what gives the hospitals the advantage when they negotiate. The emergency room physicians who did not sell out are coming under tremendous pressure from the hospitals to give up more and more. And so many of them have decided to leave the hospitals and set up free-standing emergency centers, or "walk-in" clinics. The corporations will of course beat them to the punch. Humana, for example, intends to set up six hundred such free-standing centers. The rush is on to set up these centers quickly and sell them to the highest corporate bidder.

Financial pressure is likely to send more and more emergency doctors into the corporate fold, but this time not for windfall profits but survival. The already mentioned Tax Equity and Fiscal Responsibility Act, passed by Congress in 1983, made emergency medicine a much less lucrative enterprise. TEFRA requires that hospital-based physicians submit separate bills for their professional services. No longer can hospitals submit a combined bill and remit a percentage to the physicians. The act supposedly pertains only to Medicare patients, but hospitals are applying it to nearly all patients. Emergency physicians presumably no longer collect fees on a contractual percentage basis, they collect them now on an actual basis. Emergency rooms are increasingly becoming the health provider to the poor, nonpaying customer. Whereas under the contractual agreements, hospitals underwrote part of the bad debt expected in running the service, the physicians themselves will now have to deal alone with it; on a national average at least a 25 percent decrease in income can be anticipated for them.

No doubt as the vise tightens more groups like Spectrum will come up for sale, and the mediglomerates will be very active in the ensuing transactions. For them the emergency room is still a good investment. It is pivotal to business: it fills hospital beds. A drop in income for a small group of physicians is catastrophic, but a corporation can convert that drop into a loss leader; lose a little in the emergency room and make it up once the patient is hospitalized.

It is worth noting, after all this jockeying for position and profit, that by conservative estimates 90 percent of all patients who come into an emergency room are not really very sick and needn't be there at all; they ought to be in a doctor's office, where the bill for the visit would come to $25 instead of $67. That means that of the $10 billion spent in emergency rooms in 1981, about $6 billion was wasted. It is ironic that if more doctors were available for an office visit, fewer patients would need to visit the emergency room.

It was through emergency medicine that corporations first realized that there were not only hospitals for sale but also groups of physicians for sale to work in these hospitals. But the provider-supplier circle became even tighter when the corporation acquired the medical researchers, the most basic element of all. The research side of health care constitutes medicine's invisible labyrinth—the experimental and theoretical substructure on which so much of the practice of medicine depends. By and large medical research has always been carried out by academic researchers working mostly in university hospitals and laboratories. Some large pharmaceutical companies ran their own laboratories, but the truly important work was almost always done in the universities. The work was supported for the most part by government grants and to a much smaller extent, 4 percent, by corporations, usually the large pharmaceutical concerns.

The usual practice was that a researcher in a university hospital would do his or her research and then present the useful results at a medical meeting, publishing them in a scientific journal. The old "publish or perish" rule was in effect in the universities, so that a certain amount of work could be expected from each faculty member. Most researchers were "full-time geographic," which means they were expected to spend all their time in the laboratory; for their efforts they were paid a university salary, which was generally lower than that paid to the clinical physicians. Some doctors combined research with a clinical practice and teaching, and thereby earned a little more.

The hand of the corporation, as could be expected, soon came to be felt in the research labs too, particularly in the field of genetic engineering, where in the late 1960s and 1970s great strides were being made. Working mostly at the University of California and Stanford, scientists were discovering bit by bit the methodology of genetic splicing and architecture. Genes are the hereditary building blocks of life; they are the basic organic units that pass on any inherited characteristic, such as hair and eye color, or any inherited disorder, such as Tay-Sachs disease, from parents to offspring. It is the very real possibility of interfering in a beneficial way—for example, by eliminating genetically transmitted diseases and by enhancing the reproductive probabilities of desirable characteristics—that makes genetic engineering the exciting though risky investment it is.

Traditionally a discovery made in a university laboratory under grant circumstances belongs to the researcher in name and reputation, but to the university commercially. Indeed, all major universities and medical schools maintain a patent, or "exclusive use," office to oversee the revenues from commercial ventures emanating from university-sponsored research. But in the case of genetic engineering, university scientists quickly became aware of the commercial potential of the field, and they sought private financial support as well as the usual university grants for the research they were doing. Pretty soon entire companies were formed in order to support the work of two or three investigators. Genentech is one such company that was formed in California in 1976, and matters pertaining to its relationship with Stanford University and the University of California were until recently in litigation. In 1981 Genentech went public on the over-the-counter market. The stock jumped from $35 to as high as $89 on the day of the offering. Cetus, another genetic engineering firm earlier mentioned, had a less spectacular but similarly very profitable public offering on the same market.

Despite the fact that Genentech and other companies like it are years away from marketing a salable product, their stocks are heavily traded every day. You are in essence buying shares in an idea—an idea that has the further fragility of being, in effect, a disputed piece of property. For the universities involved believe that under law they should be the sole beneficiaries of the basic discoveries of the subject, as those discoveries were made under university-administered grants on university premises. The companies involved believe on the other hand that they supported the research and that they therefore are the legitimate beneficiaries.

Regardless of the outcome of the litigation in all these cases, yet another respected boundary of medicine as it has been traditionally practiced was now irrevocably breached. For many genetic scientists soon began reporting the results of their research first to the mass media and only subsequently to the professional community. The *Wall Street Journal,* rather than the *New England Journal of Medicine,* became the forum of genetic research. When a researcher reports his or her findings in a medical journal or at a medical meeting other scientists get the chance to corroborate or dispute the findings, and maybe even take them one step further. When a genetic scientist reports his or her results to the *Wall Street Journal,* the effect of the report is essentially to push the stock of the company involved up, regardless of the opinion of other scientists on the merits of the results. And when the scientist involved also owns a company that could financially benefit from certain research findings, it is truly amazing how frequently those breakthrough findings are made in the company laboratories.

Naturally, corporate America was not going to be left off this lucrative bandwagon. Standard Oil of California got involved in, and subsequently withdrew from, a joint venture with

Cetus. Some of the large pharmaceutical companies took substantial positions in Genentech, as did some Japanese and Swedish concerns. The alliances that researchers and genetic companies thus formed have grown tremendously in a couple of years; and a large number of large corporations now have a considerable stake in what the future holds for the minuscule, manipulable gene.

It may seem odious to the general public that life-saving materials relating to the biology of existence can be privately patented at all, but the practice is worldwide and has been for over one hundred years. The institution that made the discoveries is usually protected by such patents for thirty years; then the patents expire. Even substances like penicillin and insulin were once exclusively "owned" by their discoverers. Now, however, with the shadow of Wall Street hovering over the laboratory, researchers, and corporate employees, there is a real possibility that even the medical procedures themselves, always viewed in the past as common property to be shared for the advancement of mankind, might be protected private property.

Medical procedures, such as the freezing of tissue in cancer operations to preserve the function of the diseased organ, microsurgery to restore severed limbs, and new techniques in cardiac bypass surgery, are routinely published in medical journals and texts, and taught in medical schools. But already a company called Fertility and Genetics Research is attempting to patent the procedure involved in transferring microscopic embryos from a fertile woman to an infertile one. If this company is successful, doctors who wish to use this procedure will have to obtain a special license. It is worth noting that the American Medical Association has come out strongly against this patent, which seems contrary to the public interest "since it might inhibit rapid and widespread use of a medical advance" (*Wall Street Journal,* Friday, October 21). However, as

69

the American Medical Association loses influence and political power to the large corporations, there may soon be a frightening new answer to who owns the secrets of life.

Just as emergency medicine sold out for profit, so did academic research reach for the big bucks. Never mind that reporting the results of your research in *Barron's* was diametrically opposed both to the traditions and the sensible practices of the field; if the report helped to push your stock up, then so be it. Huge profits were made when "Gene" went public—so huge in fact as to make the emergency medicine sellout appear by comparison like the takeover of the corner lemonade stand. While the shares of the jeans you were wearing went down, the shares of the gene splicers, who had no product to sell, were flying high. The new researcher-entrepreneur certainly seemed to understand the revised rules of the game. After all, *Fortune* magazine can tell if you are lying about discovering oil, but who could begin to understand all the talk about mitochondria and cell membranes.

The announcement of various cancer cures is an extreme example of the abuses inherent in presenting technical information first before an uncritical lay audience. Every so often some new or revived esoteric "cure" is paraded on the front pages of newspapers, furnishing false and cruel hope to many afflicted people. The claim of a cure is usually accompanied by the charge that the medical establishment has been trying to suppress it, because cancer research is a lucrative scam and because the disease, as long as it remains incurable, provides good income for physicians. Now it may be true that a great deal of research money is fraudulently squandered—it often, unfortunately, is. It may be true as well that doctors are all too humanly greedy (though that doesn't mean that they enjoy seeing their patients suffer and die). But it is also true that the mystery of cancer is in many ways as ineffable as the mystery of life itself, and that a cure for the disease is a profoundly intractable matter that will not yield to dollars alone. No one knows that better than the many researchers who have quietly labored outside the spotlight, trying with great effort to push back the frontiers of all we do not know just a little. If scientific finds are published in technical journals, they can be shared, tested, and, most important, used as a building block toward further research. If published elsewhere, with much information secretly guarded or misinterpreted, we are all the losers.

At any rate, the public and the investment community bought the promise that, sometime in the future, genetic engineering would prove a profitable commercial venture. Indeed a substantial, and until recently the sole, income source of Cetus was interest earned on the money the public has spent buying its shares. In this whole matter it is the issue of credibility that is a concern. Certainly there have always been scandals of research scientists "cooking" their data in order to achieve publishable, more often than not subsequently perishable, results. But in the cold light of scientific day the results are judged by other scientists. In genetic engineering, however, the new findings seem to be judged by the volatility of the stock involved, while the voice of the responsible scientific community wails unlistened to in the wilderness.

Whatever the ultimate outcome of this research, corporate business will own a dominant share, thus reinforcing the circle of influence it has secured in the medical health field. That circle now virtually encloses us in its provider-supplier grip from the moment of our birth until the final hour of life.

# 6
# OUT OF CONTROL

After their emergence, the profit-making hospital chains grew faster in the 1970s than the computer industry.

—Paul Starr
*The Social Transformation of*
*American Medicine* (1982)

As corporate luck would have it, the MIC was growing at a time when physicians were losing control of the health care system to government and private bureaucracies. The MIC is only one of the many new "controllers," but they have taken the most advantage of the increasing impotence of physicians. Certainly physicians still see the patients and prescribe pills, but their influence in shaping the important decisions in the health field is now greatly diminished.

The federal and state governments now underwrite all or part of the medical care costs for 22 percent of the American population, and for 60 percent of those older than sixty-five. That means the government foots the bill for almost every fourth patient who utilizes the health care system, and, consequently, through a myriad of imposed rules can pretty much

73

impose its will as it pleases. In California, for example, the state now determines in many instances whether or not a patient should be admitted to the hospital and to which hospital he or she may go, although it can no longer even pay the bill for services it requests. In the beginning the government said, "Do it our way or you won't get paid." Then it said, "Do it our way and you may get paid." Now it is saying, "Do it our way because that is the law."

More and more people find themselves dependent on government programs with less and less money in their budgets. As a result hospitals and physicians are caring for the sick and elderly poor without pay. It is rather difficult to run a medical practice or a hospital when the payments are always late or inadequate for 25 percent of the customers. In many states, reimbursement comes routinely six months after billing.

The result, of course, is to push more physicians and hospitals into the corporate fold. In no state do physicians have very much influence in the administration of the health care system; the programs are run by politicians and professional administrators. Totally disregarding the subtleties and complexities of the health care delivery system, the "new wave" problem solvers judge success by the decrease in the average physician's income in their state for that year. The fact that only something like two cents of every health care dollar ends up in the physician's pocket totally eludes them.

In government programs everywhere the doctor is always perceived to be the heartless profiteer. In reality, however, while health care costs exploded in 1982, the inflation rate for physicians' services slowed to 7.5 percent, a marked decrease from the 11.7 percent figure of 1981.

Government is one weighty influence in the health care system, but the private insurance carriers such as Blue Cross and Connecticut General are not far behind. Together all private health insurers provide coverage for 58 percent of the

American population. Included in this figure are all the health maintenance organizations, or HMOs, such as Kaiser-Permanente. There too physicians (with the notable exception of Kaiser) play little or no role in the direction of the organization and are often, again, perceived as the enemy. The insurance companies seem to me to play the most suspect role of all. Not a day goes by without one of them bemoaning the high costs of medical care, the burden of which, they claim, is pushing them to the brink. The last refrain in the lamentation is always a hike in subscriber fees. Essentially these companies sell expensive health care policies to the customer and then play a nerve-racking game when reimbursing the hospital and the physician. They often tell the customer they will pay for this or that, and then inform the hospital or physician that the subscriber is not covered. The behavior of these insurance companies is such that more and more physicians are demanding cash from the patient and saying, "*You* bought the policy, *you* chase Big Bear Insurance."

Indeed, many of the insurance companies hardly live up to the exalted images of themselves that they present to the public. These companies as a group control the largest cash reserves in the country, not excluding the banks. They are the largest owners of real estate in the land, bar none, and they more often than not own the largest skyscraper in a given metropolitan area as well. If anyone ever succeeds in bankrupting the health care system, in my opinion they will be the ones to do so. Their policies are very expensive, yet their payouts often do not meet their obligations. Without rhyme or reason these companies make arbitrary decisions as to which medical procedures they will pay for and which ones they will not; and very often a particular procedure is paid for in one case and not in another.

One of their ruses is the use of forms that are extremely difficult and time-consuming to fill out. It often takes three weeks after application for one of the patient's forms to arrive. It will often take three weeks after that for the physician's form to arrive. And then a full 28 percent of the completed forms are returned by the companies to the senders because of some mistake or other, necessitating a second mailing and further time delays. This means that the insurance companies have the "float" to play with while the doctors and the hospitals wait for their money or, worse still, are forced to go to the bank and finance their receivables. It is well known, for example, that American Express makes millions of dollars simply on the float from its travelers checks. To further aggravate matters, the insurance companies are now making a major effort to pre-negotiate fees with doctors and hospitals; such a practice will enhance their financial situation enormously.

Another newcomer to the health care network playing an increasingly important role is the company with a large personnel roster. It offers a choice of health plans to its employees and shops around for the least expensive policy. For them, overutilization leads to escalating costs. For example, if Big Bear Insurance spends $20 million one year in payment for health care for IBM employees, next year the company will charge IBM $25 million to underwrite coverage. Thus IBM and many other corporations have a vested interest in the cutting of health care costs. Though the general prospects for cost containment are promising, once again there is an opportunity for the MIC corporation with the largest facilities and most efficient (though not necessarily the best quality) operators to jump in and underbid all competitors. The more this happens, the more physicians and hospitals will be pushed into the MIC.

Other large corporations are actually taking the initiative and forming their own HMOs. In this case the corporations themselves pre-negotiate fees with medical providers and thus bypass the expensive middleman step. This arrangement remains probably the most cost-effective. Some banks, such as

Continental, have in fact set up self-insurance health plans for corporations that actually generate income through unused moneys judiciously invested. But unless the corporations are lucky and sign up good doctors and hospitals, the employees can get stuck with a situation of second-rate care and little choice in the matter.

Yet another element that emerged in the health care arena of the 1960s and 1970s was the growing public attention and militancy with respect to medical matters. Community and public-action groups gave the layperson new influence. For example, in the November 1982 election in Berkeley, California, a bill was passed that outlawed the use of electroconvulsive shock in city hospitals. Electroconvulsive shock may or may not be an effective therapeutic tool, but the ballot seems an unusual forum for deciding the issue. It is now conceivable that one day the citizens of Peoria, Illinois, will object to the use of penicillin in their city, and the citizens of Dubuque, Iowa, will vent their dislike of insulin in theirs.

The Berkeley ballot (which, by the way, was finally overruled by a California state judge in September 1983) is indicative of the new zeal sweeping the public. In Oakland and San Jose hundreds of people picket hospitals that perform abortions, ignoring the medical indications of the different cases. Positions on a hospital board of directors are becoming very political, and doctors and hospitals find themselves at the mercy of every new fancy that sweeps the country. The public claims that since taxpayer money supports medicine, taxpayers ought to have some say in its practice. But by its nature each medical case—each pregnancy, each emotional depression— differs from the next. It does not seem to me that the same techniques of public pressure used to persuade GM to build a safer car can also be applied to improving health care.

The women's movement has also had a tremendous impact on the practice of medicine. For the last ten years doctors and hospitals have been bombarded with the criticism that they were insensitive to the needs of women. The fact of the matter is that it is not medicine that is insensitive to women, it is some (or even many) doctors who are. Some women have decided to avoid what they consider to be the humiliating experience of the gynecological examination and to practice self-examination instead. The missed early detection of a malignancy is the price some of them may find themselves paying for such zealotry.

In the next twenty years many significant medical issues will have to be resolved: for example, just how long should life-support systems be kept going for elderly patients? Who should oversee the hospitalization of terminally ill people? How should the medical, religious, and political contradictions that surround the practice of abortion be dealt with? And we are only ten years away from facing perhaps the thorniest issues of all, those of genetic engineering. Doctors fear that their voice will be insufficiently heard when society comes to deal with these important issues.

In the 1970s, then, the medical ship was indeed sailing in rough seas. Doctors and hospitals saw the money running out, and yet they were powerless to do anything about it. Medical issues were being debated vehemently by uninformed members of the public. Most doctors agreed on the necessity for some external input, but the extent and fury of the public onslaught caught the medical community by surprise. The financial handwriting had also always been on the wall, but what hospital could have foreseen a bank considering it a poor loan risk? As helter-skelter as the health care system has always been, hospitals and physicians considered their turf sacred: they and they alone could and should make the life-and-death decisions relating to the inviolate human body. But when money ran out, the sanctity of the turf disappeared. Government, insurance companies, and the public all knew better.

In 1900 physicians comprised 90 percent of all medical and

health care workers. By 1950 they comprised only 20 percent and by 1980 they comprised only 10 percent of that population; and the percentage will in all likelihood continue to fall in the future. Medical office managers, hospital administrators, government health workers, insurance employees, claims processors, and computer programmers are all careers and professions on the rise. Phrases such as "patient mix," "cost reimbursement," "header sheets," and "profits per square foot" have become the language of the emerging army of the new healers.

In the emergency medicine field alone, we can see how physicians are greatly outnumbered. In 1982 there were 15,000 emergency room physicians who worked along with a total of one million emergency medical workers—including secretaries, nurses, paramedics, and technicians. In this field physicians now comprise only 1 percent of the work force. In 1982 there was a total of 437,688 physicians, only 4 percent of a population of ten million Americans, who derived all or part of their income from health care.

A 1983 study by the Bureau of Health Professions, Department of Health and Human Services, brought to light some very interesting numbers. Focusing on community hospitals, the study revealed a 4.9 percent increase in the number of full-time personnel employed by community hospital members of the American Hospital Association. In the period between 1980 and 1981 the number of hospital administrators jumped from 19,798 to 26,734, an increase of 25 percent. In the same period the number of doctors remained mostly constant, and the number of registered nurses increased 1.2 percent. Administrators promise to be the decade's new healers.

It is an MIC practice to raid government and insurance companies to find managers. Because of their background these managers have always had adversary relationships with physicians, and they bring this predisposition to their new corporate jobs. They are hoping the role of the licensed physician in patient treatment will continue to decrease. The passage—as of now a distinct possibility—of laws allowing physician assistants, paramedics, and nurse practitioners to exercise direct decision-making capability in the care of the patients will of course bring such a decrease about.

Despite a great decline in their effectiveness the traditional doctor and medical lobby groups still maintain some influence—due mainly, it would seem, to abundant funding and political connections. But the influence will certainly continue to decline. The American Medical Association is daily losing battles it so easily won a few years ago. As the physicians' influence recedes, that of the mediglomerate lobbies grows. Promising always to cut costs by volume, they speak the same language as the new technocrats. Professing the concern about quality, they nevertheless ignore or otherwise try to minimize the inputs of the relevant state and county medical associations.

Speaking at the annual Trustee Forum of the California Hospital Association in San Diego in the fall of 1982, Dan Smith, president of Blue Cross of California, declared that, because of the current "environment" of medicine and some recent favorable changes in the law, Blue Cross intended in the future to contract directly with doctors and hospitals for the lowest possible rates, using in its operations the so-called prudent buyer model. Mr. Smith stated that it was the economic environment that had changed, but his proposals really referred to and would never have been made but for physicians' loss of influence to the promoters of competitive, volume medicine. In a similar vein Blue Cross of New York has recently begun to offer a plan called Wraparound Plus, which links increases in doctor fees to the Consumer Price Index; here again ten thousand contracting physicians have decided they have no choice but to go along. The companies that sign the checks call the shots. The new motto is cost containment through reasonable care. Gone forever is quality, replaced by uniform standards of health care. In one annual corporate report after another the story is the same: Our low-cost methods do not affect the quality of the care delivered—in fact they may even improve it. I fear the facts are somewhat different.

Many observers agree that presently in this country an apocalyptic battle is taking place for control of the health care system. The contestants in the war, as already pointed out, include physicians, hospitals, government, and third-party payers, all striving to harness the expensive system to their own interests. It would seem that the view of Arthur Young and Company, the huge corporate accounting firm, is that the battle is over and the mediglomerates are the victors. In late January 1983 the company held its second annual health care roundtable in Palm Springs, California. The glossy report recording the proceedings tells much about how health care is perceived by the business leaders of the country. The theme of the meeting was the future of health care in this country; a prominently featured topic for discussion was "multi-institutional survival strategies." The panelists are referred to in the report as "health care industry leaders" and "acknowledged giants in the health care industry." One of those panelists was Robert W. Van Tuyle of Beverly Enterprises, the Wall Street nursing home chain that has capitalized on the graying of America and in the process made nursing homes respectable. It is pertinent to note that Arthur Young and Company serves as the accountant for Beverly, as well as for such other members of the Medical Industrial Complex as Cetus and Genentech. In any case Mr. Van Tuyle is quoted in the report as saying:

*I'd love to see a change in the law which would make it possible for us to actually employ doctors. My ideal nursing home would have the doctors in our employ routinely visiting patients like they do in acute hospitals. I would love to be able to hire those doctors and have them do a better job taking care of our patients. But legally we cannot do that now.*

Mr. Van Tuyle went on to say:

*Our market is growing tremendously and it is obvious to me that the economy cannot afford the $15 or $20 billion that will be required to build the beds to take care of the bodies. These are not assumptions, either. The bodies are already here—we are all getting older.*

Mr. Van Tuyle's comments on this occasion were out of character for this bold innovator, but they do reflect the thinking of many health care industry leaders. Physicians are looked upon as employees whose sole function is to fill the conglomerate's beds with "bodies." If the body still has disposable parts, put it for a while in a National Medical Enterprises acute care facility bed for tests and surgery (provided of course the parts are insured). When the body runs out of disposable parts, transfer it to a Hillhaven chronic care bed.

The second Palm Springs panelist was John C. Bedrosian of National Medical Enterprises. He said in part:

*A lot of people are saying that there will be serious competition and confrontation between the doctor and the hospital. I don't believe that at all. I believe the confrontation and competition will be among the physicians themselves. Young doctors are more receptive to innovation and "out-facility" activities . . .*

An "out-facility" is Wall Street jargon for a free-standing clinic, the exploitation of which NME is very interested in. Thus Mr. Bedrosian is counting on the growing physician glut to produce a professional clientele amenable to the practice of proprietary medicine. He continued:

*You have to go out and get the private patients. You have to go get your share of the market whether it is through a PPO [a preferred provider organization] or by attracting physicians into the medical building or whatever. . . . Tell the doctors: "Here you are. The rent is reasonable; now go to work."*

Who, one might well ask, does Mr. Bedrosian feel should care for the non-private patient? Or, for that matter, for the indigent patient, whose badly deteriorating prospects never seem to come up for consideration in the ongoing transformation of the health care delivery system?

The other panelists were Bernard J. Lachner, president and chief executive officer of Evanston Hospital Corporation, and Paul M. Torrens, professor of public health at UCLA. It is to be noted that not one member of the panel was a practicing physician. Executives of chain hospital companies are referred to as "leaders" and "giants" of health care, as though they alone controlled and understood the field. And although this big business takeover of medicine is now at least ten years in the process, it is occurring virtually without comment from the medical profession. The noisome silence might have something to do with the heavy advertising that MIC companies purchase in medical journals, but more likely it is a reflection of the resignation most physicians feel in their powerlessness to alter the course of affairs.

# 7
# MEDICAL
# MONOPOLY

These companies prefer to call themselves investor-owned. "Investor-owned" is to "in business for profit" as "Department of Defense" is to "Department of War"—a semantic device to obscure their true function.

—H. JACK GEIGER, M.D.
City University of New York (1983)

Anecdotal hospital horror stories are abundant everywhere and, indeed, have been the subject of many books. From a physician's point of view, these grisly tales of incompetence and suffering always seem to occur at "St. Elsewhere," only in rare cases at one's own hospital. The stories are a sad and sometimes inevitable feature of an arena of life involving frightened, sick patients and health care professionals who make, alas, all too frequently all too human mistakes. Over the years I have collected such stories along with everyone else; but I feel that the unfortunate events related happen with about the same frequency in all types of facilities, whether for profit or no. Their occasional and unpredictable occurrence is not what distinguishes the two different systems of health care delivery; it is something far more basic.

The truth is that when a for-profit public corporation (as opposed to, say, a for-profit private individual) takes over the ownership of a hospital, a subtle yet profound change takes place in the entire system of health care dispensation. The change is systematic, unavoidable. It is this fact that seems to me overlooked in all the largely enthusiastic literature about the emergent MIC. It is not merely that a self-interested acquisitive dimension now comes to pervade the system; quite the contrary, medicine has always handsomely rewarded its practitioners and has thus attracted many a doctor who cannot clearly read an X-ray for the dancing dollar signs blurring his vision. No, the reasons have something to do with the entire network of decision making—decision making on the highest level and therefore affecting the very nature of the practice of medicine in the land—being shifted from within the professional domain itself to the backrooms, usually the accounting rooms, of corporate command.

I do not claim that the American Medical Association is not avaricious, or that physicians are opposed to their own wealth and comfort. Nevertheless—and despite their inexcusable excesses—the decisions made by doctors, singly or in concert, take cognizance of, by virtue of many long years of arduous training and experience, the special exigencies of responsible medical practice. The philosopher Albert R. Jonsen, a long-time "doctor watcher," recently wrote an article asserting that the "central paradox" of a physician's life was the conflict between self-interest and altruism. Consider now what must happen when decision making is given over to a person whose main concern is efficient administration and cost containment—all with a view to end-of-quarter profits.

As *Newsweek* reports (October 31, 1983), one result of such a shift can be seen in the failure of Humana Corporation to set up what it considered an unprofitable adult burn unit at their hospital in Louisville, Kentucky, despite the fact that no other such unit was available in the city. It took the public outcry over the death of a burn victim who might have been saved to convince them to reverse their decision. Consider furthermore what must happen when the hospital owner also owns a few bowling alleys or a fast-food chain, and the hospital profits are routinely merged with the profits from the other, nonmedical concerns. In such a situation a possible boardroom discussion could involve a decision to sell the hospital in order to buy another bowling alley (this after an extensive advertising campaign has failed to produce more work for the hospital's underemployed cosmetic surgeon), or vice versa. It seems evident to me that a serious problem with serious ramifications for everyone is involved here. And the most puzzling paradox of all is that it is the public ownership of the companies and the free trade of their shares in the stock markets of the country that have created the problem.

It does take the breath away—at least it takes away mine—to see clearly that, in the present state of affairs, the profits gained from the practice of medicine appear to show up in the pockets of stock market speculators—a particularly unpleasant instance, in my opinion, of illicit fee splitting. It is illegal in every state of the country for a physician to pay out to anyone moneys proportional to the volume of his practice; the inevitable consequences of the present system seem to me to violate the spirit if not the letter of the law.

More important, the corporate complex as a whole raises serious worries because of its nature and size. In effect five hundred listed corporations have developed the infrastructure of a privately planned health care system that already owns a sizable percentage of both the acute beds and the chronic beds of the hospital facilities in this country, and also supplies almost all the goods and materials to support the system. While capturing a full one-third of every health care dollar, the complex really operates outside the usual health care controlling mechanisms.

If these corporate entities were independent, autonomous

companies each competing with the others, there would be less cause for concern. The problem is, however, that they are often closely interrelated in not always perceivable ways by common ownership of stock, shared board members, frequent instances of joint ventures and frequent transactions among themselves. They are sympathetically aware of one another, whether they are obviously competing or not, and the consequences for the public are not always happy ones.

The mode of operation of hospital chains is, as I've noted, always the same: buy or build a facility in a nice suburb, attract as many doctors to the area as possible, and overutilize the facility as much as possible. There is not a medical journal around that is not filled with advertisements from the chains for doctors to relocate to their particular area. Besides advertising for doctors, the corporate chains also heavily advertise for patients, playing on human anxieties to encourage unnecessary but lucrative procedures such as face-lifts and breast enlargements. In Albuquerque, New Mexico, a well-known obstetrician/gynecologist advertises his practice from a hot-air balloon shaped like a stork. His local hospital, Lovelace Medical Center, describes itself in the newspaper as "an alternative way to bring life into the world in a joyous manner at a reasonable price."

In a 1983 article in the *Journal of the American Medical Association,* Richard A. Wright and Bruce H. Allen write that the medical advertising will not benefit the profession in any way— i.e., it will not lower costs and it will not increase physicians' incomes—but it cannot be entirely avoided either, because of the marketing and advertising wizardry of the mediglomerates (a neologism of their coining). The history of health care advertising in general is replete with notorious cases of need created where none existed before—such as for vaginal sprays and "tummy tucks"—which often created more problems than they remedied. An executive of a well-known ad agency has proudly claimed that he conceived the idea of a vaginal deodorant and took it to a pharmaceutical company. Subsequently vaginal deodorants did sell very well for many companies but some were later found to contain carcinogens.

Moreover, since these corporations thrive on overutilization, they must certainly take some blame for rising health costs. Indeed, someone must pay the bill for their advertising too. And despite their obvious know-how at running a certain type of facility, they have contributed nothing to the betterment of the system in general.

Many people in the past have tried to compare quality in health facilities but none have really succeeded—it is not an easy thing to do. What can be said is that the chain facilities strive for fewer personnel per shift per ward in order to save money. *Newsweek* (October 31, 1983) reports that "National Medical Enterprises has cut the number of licensed registered nurses from 40 percent of staff to 25 percent and are hiring as many lower-paid aides and other unlicensed medical workers as possible." In general, you turn a profit, where others have failed, by cutting corners; the rounded corners cannot be seen from the outside. It is also known that the chains skimp on their hospital-based physicians such as emergency physicians, radiologists, and pathologists, and it is these hospital-based physicians that really determine the quality of an institution. In medicine as in everything else, you get what you pay for.

All the same, it has always been thought that chain hospitals had grown so rapidly and become so successful because they had achieved efficiency through volume. The public, the media, physicians, and investors all bought the line, and in a sense much of the Wall Street maneuvering was overlooked in deference to companies that supposedly were contributing to cost containment. The myth, however, was exploded recently by the publication in August 1983 in the *New England Journal of Medicine* of an elaborate study carried out by Robert V. Pattison and H. M. Katz that showed that (at least in California) the proprietary chains charged patients an average of 24 percent more than the nonprofits did for the same services. The study also considered the fee schedules of seventy-eight for-profit independent California hospitals, and found that the chains also billed more than these facilities. The higher costs often appeared in the higher charges for drugs (priced for a profit margin of 80% vs 20% at not-for-profit hospitals), laboratory tests, and X-rays. Thus not only are the chains overutilizing, they are doing so at inflated prices.

Prior to the appearance of Pattison and Katz's article, the corporate chains had always claimed they were cheaper. Now in response to the article Michael Bromberg, director of the Federation of American Hospitals, a Washington-based trade group of investor-owned hospitals, was quoted as saying: "You can't be both newer and cheaper and we've never said we're cheaper." The statement is in direct contradiction to a truckload of corporate annual reports dating back fifteen years, right up to the present. Americans have until now granted listed corporations license to own so many hospitals because they believed the Madison Avenue glossies extolling the virtues of volume and efficiency as a potent cost-containment mechanism. The Pattison and Katz study is significant because it established for the first time that the chaining of hospitals under corporate umbrellas has actually led to the escalation of health costs rather than the cutting down. More recently still (*Barron's*, October 17, 1983), the influential financial writer Alan Abelson accused the larger chains of expanding for the sole purpose of receiving increased depreciation reimbursements from the federal government. Therein also lies the partial answer to how these companies have grown so rich so quickly while so many other hospitals were dying. If every gambler who claimed to be a winner were, there would not be a casino left on the Las Vegas strip. If all the chain hospitals were as cost efficient as they claimed, not a single one of them would be listed on a stock exchange.

Suppose you were a forty-year-old jogger who developed chest pains and you showed up at a National Medical Enterprises hospital in Los Angeles. Based on the usual treatment for chest pains of this nature and the average bill for the common tests involved, you would be given an examination, an electrocardiogram, a chest X-ray, blood tests, and a few hours of observation on a monitor. In all you would spend three hours in the emergency room and be given a bill of $410. You would also have a 50 percent chance of being admitted to the coronary care unit for three to five days' observation, costing a further $3,600. If on the other hand you were to show up in the emergency room of the Stanford University Medical Center, your emergency room bill would be 24 percent lower and there would be only a 25 percent likelihood of hospital admission. The difference comes about because the Stanford physicians are a touch more discerning and have no vested interest in hospital admissions. For the fact is, *quality* medical care *cuts* medical costs. Astute independent clinicians save billions in avoiding needless tests and hospitalizations. The corporations make money while Stanford does not because Stanford charges you less and provides more.

A word about volume. In medicine, unlike the clothing business, there really is not that much cost efficiency to be gained by high volume. I do not care how thin you slice it, the cost of running two hospitals is roughly double that of running one. (And if hospital chains have been saving money on volume buying and equipment sharing, the Pattison and Katz study definitely shows these savings are not passed on to patients.) It costs twice as much to care for ten multiple trauma cases properly as it does for five. In my opinion it simply is not true that you can operate fifty hospitals more cheaply if there is a single owner. That is, of course, if you do not do what Petrolane was accused of doing with its twenty-four Raleigh Hills alcohol rehabilitation centers, when it shuttled patients in its facilities across state lines in order to avoid state limits on Medicare coverage.

Every reputable hospital in the country knows that caring for alcoholics is "bad business." Treatment calls for long-term care and for expensive medical, social, and psychological expertise. In short, it is difficult to make a profit caring for alcoholics, but Petrolane showed how it could be done. And when American Medical International, a New York Stock Exchange company, bought Petrolane's twenty-four Raleigh Hills facilities to add to its chain of seventy-four hospitals, it did so to add to its stable of 9,713 licensed beds. The company does not have a special interest in alcoholism, nor does it have a single physician on its board. Petrolane's troubles made a medical bargain available, and AMI jumped at the opportunity. So anxious are these operators to treat alcoholics that *Newsweek* (October 31, 1983) reports they will "make marketing calls to judges, lawyers, social service agencies," anyone who has contact with alcoholics.

As for the ability of the mediglomerates to reduce waste, on July 21, 1983, the congressional subcommittee studying health and long-term health care cited figures indicating that Americans spend $10 billion a year on over-the-counter drugs, 40 percent of which contain unlisted ingredients. It was estimated that $21 billion is lost each year to unnecessary drug-related hospitalizations. The mediglomerates profit from the consumption of these products and then again on the drug-related hospitalizations.

Yet, strangely enough, a recent Harris Poll cited in *Business Week* asking people who they thought was responsible for increasing health costs showed most believed it was villainous, wasteful doctors who were running expensive hospitals. In fact few doctors own hospitals and even fewer run them. None of the choices the respondents were given to tick off mentioned either corporate ownership of hospitals or advertising leading to overutilization. The omission is puzzling inasmuch as the poll appears as part of a feature story describing corporate ownership of hospitals.

While they continue to claim greater efficiency, the mediglomerates are generally sensitive to criticisms of quality and costs. A recent annual report issued by Humana states: "Our record of providing the highest quality hospital care is not . . . well known." The actual quality of some Humana hospitals may rightly be questioned in my opinion since recently, and for the first time, the company added a physician to the corporate management team that consults with each Humana hospital prior to the visitation by a team from the Joint Commission on Accreditation of Hospitals. So from 1968, when the company went public, until 1981 (and then only because of a fear of losing the necessary accreditations), no physician was involved as an officer of the corporation in overseeing quality control in Humana hospitals. Humana considers the addition of a physician to that process a "significant step in quality measurement"; I would have thought it would have expressed embarrassment that for so many years no physician's presence was deemed necessary. The magnitude of the oversight becomes all the clearer when you consider that there are an astounding eighteen thousand physicians who practice medicine within Humana hospitals.

The decision-making process in chain facilities obviously places less emphasis on local personal needs compared to global corporate interests. Each local administrator is given a budget and in effect is told to practice the best type of medicine at the least cost. His or her main concern is to produce good numbers for the head office. Good numbers mean promotion; poor numbers mean failure. The danger in all this is that while the corporations require a certificate of need from the community

in order to buy or build a hospital, they can subsequently pull
the plug at any time—that is, they are free to close the hospital
or a particular unit whenever they choose, despite the needs of
the community that has come to depend on them.

Chaining of facilities allows for abuses such as Petrolane's
alleged shuttling of patients between its facilities in order to
avoid ceilings on patient payments. A similar danger exists
with Hospital Corporation of America, the largest acute bed
owner, owning 20 percent of Beverly Enterprises, the dominant chronic care bed owner. Recall also Beverly's new joint
venture with Upjohn in the home care field. Patients could
conceivably be shuttled efficiently from acute care facility to
chronic care facility, all under the same corporate umbrella. In
addition, the corporate administration can choose to institu-
tionalize the patient in the type of facility that maximizes
insurance reimbursement, regardless of the patient's specific
health needs.

Yet the extent of the interrelationships of the MIC companies has received little attention. In 1975 for the first time, the
Supreme Court, in *Goldfarb* v. *Virginia State Bar,* 421 U.S. 773,
ruled that the learned professions were not exempt from the
jurisdiction of the Sherman Antitrust Act.

Then, in 1977 the Ninth Circuit Court of Appeals in
*Boddicker* v. *Arizona State Dental Association,* 549 F.2d 626, ruled:

> *To survive a Sherman Act challenge a particular practice, rule or
> regulation of a profession . . . must serve the purpose for which the
> profession exists, viz. to serve the public. Those which only supress
> competition between practitioners will fail to survive the challenge.*

The Sherman Act prohibits all unreasonable anticompetitive
practices, and some, such as price fixing allocation of customers, tying agreements, etc., are deemed to be per se illegal
" . . . Because their pernicious effect on competition and lack of
any redeeming virtue are conclusively presumed to be unreasonable and therefore illegal without elaborate inquiry as to the

94

precise harm they have caused or the business excuse for their use." (U.S. Supreme Court: *Northern Pacific RY* v. *United States,* 356 U.S. 1, 5 [1958].)

The listed corporations involved in health care are certainly commercial ventures involved in interstate commerce, and as such are subject to the provisions of the Sherman Antitrust Act. I submit that a great many of the activities of these corporations unreasonably restrict trade and have a "pernicious effect on competition and lack any redeeming virtue." Whether the courts will also find them "unreasonable and therefore illegal" remains to be seen.

The goal of the corporations, then, is to make health care just another consumable service that they provide for a profit. However, what is good for General Motors may not necessarily be good for the sick patient. General Motors first sells you a car, then sells you financing for that car, and finally sells you parts to replace the worn ones. The MIC gets you into the system by selling you a doctor. That doctor, acting in concert with the complex, then sells you the X-rays, laboratory tests, medicines, and a hospital bed, along with the complex's hospital linens and food. The result of all this may be needless visits to the doctor, an excess of expensive tests, and unnecessary hospitalizations. Too many health dollars being spent enriches the complex but bankrupts the individual and the public.

For the medical profession this era may well be one of the most shameful and ethically questionable periods in its history. For all of us it is a really sad time, the passing of virtually a whole other way of life. The encounter between physician and patient used to involve a sacred trust. A physician was one of the few people one could confide in, sure he had nothing but one's best interests at heart. Certainly there have always been some doctors who abused this privilege. But in a serious sense the exceptions proved the rule. The majority of doctors believe in the sacred doctor-patient trust, a bond that traditionally and

95

historically transcended all other interests. Even legally a doctor-patient relationship has a special status. Now, what is the patient to think when his doctor's office is located within a hospital owned by a corporation listed on the New York Stock Exchange?

The vast majority of people do not even know that a major change in the system of health care delivery has taken place. Indeed the majority of patients admitted to a hospital do not know who really owns it. Many shareholders of Humana and National Medical Enterprises do not realize that "their" companies may be practicing medicine. Suffice it to say that the companies themselves do not blatantly publicize the matter because of the possible legal ramifications. When Humana acquired Emergency Medical Services, the fact never saw light of day in its annual report. Whereas most companies list the earnings of their subsidiaries separately, ARA buries the earnings of Spectrum Emergency Care among other figures. Eager as these corporations are to enter the health care field, they are sometimes somewhat hesitant to publicize the details.

The Medical Industrial Complex presents society with several moral and practical dilemmas, not the least of which is whether it should be allowed to exist at all. Corporations by their nature are bottom-line creatures whose sole organizational purpose is the creation of profits for their shareholders. In health care, however, that bottom line should be sacrificed in order to ensure the highest-quality care. Cynics will say that the ideal is rarely achieved but certainly most health care providers aspire to it and make a genuine effort to achieve it. In all my experience in private, county, and academic hospitals, I have never seen a sick patient turned away for economic reasons. Yes, a power-drunk administrator may have gotten away once with such an act. But as a rule it doesn't happen, and no hospital board in the country would allow it to happen twice in its hospitals.

Corporations may not understand this "bad business" of selling even if the buyer can't pay. They don't understand the deep commitment that medicine has to reducing pain, alleviating suffering, and giving comfort to the sick. The financial rewards of health care are generous, but they are outstripped by the great satisfaction one receives by helping, by just being there when one is needed. Corporations do not understand the joy of working through a very difficult case and achieving a cure, and they will never understand the dejection that comes with failure.

Physicians who work for or work with a major corporation of the MIC must deal with a significant conflict of interest, as Arnold Relman pointed out in his celebrated article on the subject. Physicians who sell themselves to corporate buyers open major ethical issues. The act of selling a medical practice to a corporation may be unethical because you are selling the trust and goodwill of your patients. Camouflaging the sale by selling "contracts" does not improve the ethics.

I question whether listed corporations should have been allowed to acquire strings of hospitals without so much as a rudimentary public debate or discussion of the issues. Make no mistake about it: any corporation that owns a hospital and either employs physicians or contracts with them to work in that hospital is practicing medicine. If said physician does not order enough expensive tests or hospitalize enough patients, the corporation will dismiss that physician and find a replacement who will. A recent article in *Medical Economics* states that "Hospitals are now practicing medicine and they're getting more deeply into it every day. They clearly intend to take over from the private practitioner." When strings of hospitals are owned by a corporation, by inference it is the corporation that is practicing medicine.

Not satisfied with hospitals alone, these corporations are now making a concentrated effort to put even your family doctor out of business. Humana, for example, is planning to open six hundred "walk-in" clinics across the country to capture yet another fixture of the health market; shades, one might think, of Burger King. It is illegal for a professional entity to practice medicine across state lines but Humana has set up partnerships in each state in order to do so. These clinics can charge a lot less than the general practitioner because Humana and its franchised MedFirst operators will choose from the growing glut of physicians to staff them. The physicians will have little to say in the decisions that are made.

More important, while executives of health corporations and commentators delight in referring to the chain hospitals as the McDonald's of health care, there is a crucial fact they are all forgetting. Health care represents an essential service. If you don't like the fact that Pillsbury owns Burger King you can eat at your local greasy spoon. As a matter of fact, you can go an entire lifetime without ever consuming a Wendy's hamburger but you have little chance of lasting through three score and ten without visiting a hospital. When you total your car on the freeway or get hit in the head by a baseball you will be brought to the nearest hospital, without much to say in the matter.

I am offended by the cynical view of medicine put forth by the MIC. They say medicine is nothing more than a business to generate profits. The large university teaching and research hospitals offer a different point of view. They do not and cannot base their success or failure on whether they show a profit.

A brief look at the problems facing the 123 academic health centers across the country will help explain in part why proprietary hospitals have been so financially successful.

In a 1981 survey know as the Yale-New Haven Hospital Study, types of hospitals were classified as follows:

1. primary teaching hospitals;

2. hospitals with medical school affiliation and residency programs;
3. unaffiliated hospitals with residency programs; and
4. hospitals not involved in any teaching.

The study found that average total expenditures were highest in primary teaching hospitals and decreased in the second through fourth types. The primary teaching hospitals steadily show the least profit, yet they clearly make the greatest contribution to the health care system.

The primary teaching hospitals are often in inner-city areas and care for a large number of medically indigent patients. The nation's teaching hospitals represent 18 percent of the nation's beds but sustain 35 percent average deductions for bad debt and 47 percent for charity. In addition, patients who are sicker and who require complicated care are more likely to be referred to a teaching hospital. The interns, residents, and medical students represent an added expense.

The MIC has concentrated on exactly the opposite pole of health care. Its hospitals are for the most part nonteaching suburban centers with insured patients who have relatively simple problems (although HCA is about to acquire two psychiatric hospitals with university affiliation).

The corporations conquered because over the last twenty years everyone else fouled up. Government, the medical profession, insurance companies, and the so-called health experts and consultants had produced a money-sapping monster that only euphemistically could be referred to as a health care system. The corporations bit off a chunk of the system and made it work. Spurred on by greed and acquisitiveness they showed how to turn a profit pushing hospital beds. Woe to the medical profession. Woe to the patient. Woe to the country.

# 8
# SOME OF THE PLAYERS

Traditionally health care has been controlled by physicians. The control originated in the mystery and fears associated with illness and dying, [and] is fed by technology.

—VICTOR FUCHS
Professor of Economics
Stanford University

Of the approximately five hundred listed companies that can be said to form the Medical Industrial Complex, I have chosen to discuss about thirty-five, for purposes of illustration. The companies I note are not necessarily the largest; but in their various activities and aggressivity they exercise a profound influence on the new system of health care delivery.

The companies provide examples of all facets of the new medical business. Some own hospitals; some own hospitals and doctor contracts; some build hospitals; some supply hospitals with food and linens; some provide hospitals with financial services; some operate health maintenance organizations; and still others provide private health insurance. All of the companies derive all or significant portions of their revenues from the delivery of health care services or support others in delivering these services and in all fairness a few do have a genuine sense of social responsibility. The presence on the list of such companies as Sears or IBM will surprise, but I shall justify their inclusion by demonstrating the important role that they play within the MIC.

Blue Cross and Kaiser are not listed companies, but they are included here because of their importance in the overall medical picture. Blue Cross is the largest health insurer in the country; Kaiser runs the most successful health maintenance organization in the country. These organizations continue to exercise influence on the MIC.

## ARA SERVICES

ARA Services, founded in Philadelphia by D. Davidson in 1959, is now one of the largest food service companies in the country. It also supplies other goods and services to health care facilities, educational institutions, and a wide variety of industries. ARA Services reaches ten million Americans every day of the year. The company is the largest distributor of periodicals in the country and the largest national school bus operator, transporting 500,000 students each day. ARA is the nation's largest garment and textile rental firm, providing more uniforms than the U.S. Army. The company began simply as a supplier of vending machines to hospital waiting rooms and cafeterias, but it soon branched out to a remarkable degree. It is ARA that recently purchased Spectrum Emergency Care, the emergency physicians partnership. Spectrum now contracts with 250 hospitals in the United States. Spectrum itself is branching out; one of its new divisions, Correctional Medical Systems, contracts to supply physicians to prisons.

Food and refreshment account for 56 percent of ARA's revenues and 41 percent of ARA's profits; its health care operations account for 10 percent of revenues and 14 percent of profits. Health care thus returns the company a higher proportion of profit than food services do, and the purchase of Spectrum was intended to bolster that line of business.

ARA, in addition, is the second-largest operator of skilled nursing homes in the country. It achieved that distinction by acquiring, between 1973 and 1976, National Living Centers, Geriatrics, and Western Medical Enterprises. ARA now operates 260 long-term care facilities and retirement centers with 31,000 beds in ten states.

The ARA credo can virtually be stated: Since we already supply food and linens to hospitals, we will supply doctors as well. But there are ethical questions involved when many of Spectrum's doctors work at and admit patients to hospitals supplied by ARA food and ARA linens. A physician is supposed to be delivering health care, not food and linens, to patients.

It seems to me unethical and probably illegal for the profits derived from Spectrum's practice of medicine to appear in the pockets of the more than 14,000 ARA shareholders. No matter how you camouflage it, a form of fee splitting may be involved. Through a multitude of professional partnerships set up in various states, Spectrum and the parent ARA are in effect practicing medicine across state lines. While staying within the bounds of corporate law, ARA is pushing medical ethics and licensing statutes to the limit.

It is ironic to note that the Department of Justice investigated ARA's acquisition of Means Services Inc., a uniform-rental business, for possible antitrust violations while ignoring its other, more significant activities.

ARA believes that, "Because the world will never outgrow its need for service," the company's fortunes are assured. The same company that pushes vending machines now pushes doctors. It is conceivable that one day it will develop a vending machine with a doctor inside to dispense hot or cold penicillin.

There are 11.5 million shares of ARA Services, of which institutions own 49 percent. For 1982, revenues were $2.8 billion with net income of $43.8 million. Earnings for 1983 are expected to rise 20 percent over the depressed $3.65 per share in 1982. ARA has 115,000 employees. *Fortune* magazine ranks ARA twenty-ninth in its listing of the fifty largest retailing companies. Even though ARA is one of the few companies that actually owns a physician group, *Fortune* does not rank them with the diversified service companies such as HCA and Humana. The purchase of a professional medical group by a listed corporation is the ultimate expression of the industrialization of the health care system. A mere twenty years ago such a transaction would have been unheard of. It is thus not only the financial details and systems that have changed but the entire atmosphere. As in many other spheres of life, yesterday's taboos are today's common practices.

## CONNECTICUT GENERAL INSURANCE
## INA CORPORATION
## CIGNA CORPORATION

Connecticut General Insurance is the holding company for Connecticut General Life Insurance and Aetna Insurance. In April 1981 the shareholders of the parent company approved a proposal to convert Connecticut General into a general business corporation, thus allowing it to expand and diversify.

For the year ending December 1980, net income for Connecticut General was $330 million, with total assets of $16,741,000,000. There are 41,328,827 shares in the company, and in 1981 each share earned $8.20. Connecticut General is the eighth-largest life and health insurer and twenty-fourth-largest property-casualty insurer in the country.

Connecticut General became a major factor in the health

care field when it merged with INA in 1982. The new entity, CIGNA, thus became the operator of the second-largest HMO in the country. Obviously, Connecticut General, with its enormous assets, would become a major factor in whatever field it chose to enter.

INA Corporation, one of the country's largest financial services companies, dates back to 1792. With its principal subsidiary, Insurance Company of North America, it is one of the nation's largest insurance organizations. A new health care division of the company has been expanding rapidly through acquisitions.

INA acquired Ross-Loos of southern California, essentially a physician group. In November 1980, INA bought the 93-bed Beaumont Neurological Center in Texas for $8 million. In October of the same year the company acquired American Health Services Inc. for $17 million, and thus became the owner of four psychiatric hospitals. In addition, the company acquired a 40 percent interest in Mount Elizabeth Hospital in Singapore for $18 million. And in September 1981, the company purchased St. Augustine General Hospital in Florida for $10 million, thus acquiring 115 more beds.

Health care operations earned INA $553 million in 1980, but profits have clearly been much higher since. Together with Connecticut General, INA operates the INA prepaid HMOs. These two insurance giants have enormous assets (pooled, they would be truly enormous) and are extremely aggressive. Their relationship, coupled with their predilection for the HMO concept, probably indicates that they will continue acquiring various struggling companies in the future. ARA is content to own doctors and provide services to hospitals. Connecticut General and INA seem to want it all: doctors, hospitals, HMOs, and insurers.

As insurance companies, both Connecticut General and INA have tremendous assets to invest. INA Capital Management Corporation, a subsidiary of INA that does the investing for the company, holds substantial positions in Humana, Hospital Corporation of America, National Medical Enterprises, and Beverly Enterprises.

The lines of ownership and competition in all these transactions leave much to be desired. Two insurance giants own a group of physicians and operate the second-largest HMO in the country. One of the insurers has a subsidiary that invests in other listed medical companies which themselves own doctors and hospitals. Theoretically all these insurers and hospital owners should be competing with each other, but the practice would seem to be much different. To say the least, the General Motors of the health industry is *not* competing against Ford.

The stage is set for CIGNA to emerge as one of the most powerful members of the MIC. There will be no hospital in the country too expensive for the conglomerate to acquire. There will be no HMO in the country that will be able to compete with the giant in the field, should the giant decide on a competitive showdown. An obvious target will be the number one organization in the field, Kaiser-Permanente, about which, more later. If CIGNA finds that it cannot compete with Kaiser, it will buy out Kaiser.

CIGNA is now the third-largest diversified financial company, ranked by assets. In 1982 the company had revenues of $11.7 billion and a net income of $516.9 million.

## LIFEMARK CORPORATION

Lifemark, based in Houston, Texas, and run by W. S. Mackey, Jr., and P. M. Frison, owns or leases twenty-five hospitals with a total of 3,725 beds. The company also manages (for their noncorporate owners) ten hospitals with 838 beds, under contracts that give Lifemark a monthly base fee and a percentage of revenues or profits. The company also plans, develops, and constructs new hospitals.

Lifemark also provides contract respiratory therapy services in eighteen unaffiliated units, manages eight hospital pharmacies, provides physical therapy under contract to twelve hospitals, and owns a chain of dental laboratories.

For the year 1981 the company had revenues of $273 million and a net income of $18.4 million. The company has 11,463,000 shares, of which institutions, mainly insurance companies, own 41 percent.

Lifemark is a prime example of an aggressive successful corporate health care entity. The company first buys hospitals and then attracts doctors to fill the hospital beds.

To underline its aggressive posture, Lifemark, in June 1982, sold $25 million of 11 percent subordinated debentures, due 2002, convertible into common at $33 per share. The company states that proceeds of this sale will be used to finance acquisition programs, which means the buying of more hospitals.

Lifemark, with its thirty-five owned or managed hospitals, is certainly not a giant in the field; but its aggressive style of attracting physicians to its hospitals has met with remarkable success. Most of the hospitals are not in very desirable locations, but the company promises interested physicians the moon, and usually delivers.

No medical journal in the land is published without some entreaty from Lifemark seeking physicians for various positions. The likelihood is that Lifemark will substantially increase its stable of Texas hospitals over the next five years. This goal should not be too difficult to achieve, since just about every second Texas hospital is for sale.

Earnings for 1983 are expected to rise to about $2.75 a share, up from $2.30 for 1982. The company is thriving, but appears to lack the resources to expand as rapidly as its major competitors.

The fifth-largest hospital management concern in the country, Lifemark had often been viewed as a takeover candidate. And in fact in October 1983 the company announced that it was talking to both Hospital Corporation of America and American Medical International about being acquired. A week or so later Lifemark announced that it had merged with American Medical International in a $1 billion transaction. The combined company thus became the second-largest owner of acute beds in the land, after Hospital Corporation of America.

Personally I believe that Lifemark foresaw a cloudy future for itself in the light of the new Medicare prospective payments regulations and wanted to bail out while it was still prospering. The period of consolidation within the industry is about to begin. The only survivors may well be a few giant corporations, commanding huge resources, that at this moment are perhaps not even involved in health care at all.

## NATIONAL MEDICAL ENTERPRISES

NME, the fifth-largest acute care chain in the country, is the typical example of how a health care company can become the darling of Wall Street while maintaining a questionable reputation among many physicians, to put it politely, within the medical community. The company exemplifies to me just about everything that is questionable about a corporate entity in the medical business. As already pointed out, NME was founded in the late 1960s by three lawyers, Eamer, Bedrosian, and Cohen, in order to raise capital for some of their client hospitals. Operating out of Los Angeles, the legal trio successfully followed Thomas Frist's HCA methodology and themselves created a corporate medical empire.

For 1982 NME had a net income of $75.2 million on revenues of $1.2 billion. In 1982 each of the company's 46,887,826 shares earned $2 for the 13,752 shareholders of record. Thirty-one percent of the company's shares are owned by institutions. Revenues for fiscal 1983 rose another 35 percent as a result of strong demand and higher prices.

NME is a California-based hospital management company that has compiled a sterling financial growth record, to the delight of investors everywhere. It is the third-largest acute and chronic chain hospital company in the country. This was accomplished by adding hospitals, developing existing facilities, and aggressively expanding other health care services.

General hospitals account for 61 percent of revenues and 66 percent of profits, and skilled nursing facilities contribute 20 percent of revenues and 18 percent of profits. As of 1982 the company owned thirty-seven acute care hospitals with 5,445 beds and managed for others sixteen acute care hospitals with 1,825 beds. The company also owns 159 skilled nursing facilities with 18,906 beds, eight home health agencies, ninety hemodialysis stations, and seventy-six Medi-$ave pharmacies. Its subsidiaries include Livingston Medical Products Company, Hospital Pulmonary Services, Stolte Inc., T.A.D., and Avanti Inc.

In March 1982, NME bought National Health Enterprises, a listed company that operates sixty-five long-term care facilities, for $100 million cash. In April 1982 NME acquired First Washington Group, Inc., the operator of twenty-one psychiatric hospitals, for another $100 million cash. In May 1982 NME signed two long-term leases to manage two hospitals in Texas and one in North Carolina.

Investment analysts point to NME's impressive growth record as proof that medicine is a good business. Physicians who work in NME facilities will, on the other hand, point out that good business does not necessarily mean good care. For the truth of the matter is that the practices of NME illustrate how you can always squeeze profits out of a health care operation if you are calculating enough. The modus operandi of the company rarely deviates from the plan: Buy a hospital at a low cost because the previous owner was running it at a loss;

then maximize utilization, cut expenses, and raise the prices to patients. You accomplish this by the aggressive recruitment of physicians who will fill the hospital beds and use the laboratory, X-ray, surgical, and pharmacy facilities; cut corners in personnel, and pay less for hospital-based physicians. Thus emergency physicians, radiologists, and pathologists earn lower incomes at NME facilities than in just about any other medical operation.

NME does not seem to recognize the fact that the quality of hospital-based physicians determines the quality of the hospital. And regardless of the quality of the general medical staff, a poor pathology department—which, being responsible for the examination of surgical tissue and the review of hospital deaths, is at the core of the hospital operation—makes for a poor hospital.

The typical NME skeleton hospital has just enough meat on it to receive the blessing of the Joint Commission on Accreditation of Hospitals. Its records, nursing staff coverage, and procedure manuals meet all requirements but never excel. Such a hospital may be adequate for the everyday minor maladies, but one would probably not want to find oneself in an NME facility with a serious or complicated medical problem. The NME hospital administrator appears to be a typical corporate manager whose main interest is the production of good numbers for the head office in Los Angeles.

Orders come down through several bureaucratic levels. In general the theme is: Practice the best medicine you can for the least amount of money. In my opinion, their formula is: Do anything it takes to fill the beds with bodies and keep the bodies alive long enough to rack up a hefty bill for Blue Cross or Medicaid. A good doctor by NME standards is one who fills beds and overutilizes X-ray and laboratory facilities. Glorious as its reputation is on Wall Street, it is often criticized in the medical community.

110

Now another danger presents itself—the imminent participation of NME in HMO programs, which will leave many an unlucky employee subscriber with little choice but to use an NME hospital. With giants such as Connecticut General and INA having the option of owning shares in NME, the possibility is all the more likely.

The typical NME hospital seems to me to have a Hilton exterior with a Motel Six interior. It looks like a hospital and has all the trappings, but where it really counts, there are deficiencies—fewer nurses per shift per ward, questionable quality of some hospital-based physicians, pathologists, and radiologists. And always present is that fixed hallmark of chain hospital medicine, overutilization.

National Medical Enterprises has 40,100 employees. *Fortune* magazine ranks it forty-sixth in their listing of the one hundred largest service companies. In 1981 NME had not yet made the list; two years of rapid growth later, it had arrived with a bang.

## HUMANA

Humana is the thirty-sixth-largest diversified service company (ranked by sales) and the third-largest acute chain hospital company in the United States, behind only HCA and the merged AMI-Lifemark. It is listed on the New York Stock Exchange and is another health care darling of Wall Street. Operating out of Louisville, Kentucky, Wendell Cherry and David A. Jones have established Humana as one of the premier listed chain health facility companies. In October 1981 the company declared that it would spend $43 million in 1982 to open a string of free-standing medical centers for the treatment of minor emergencies. The plan was to build sixty-six centers in fifteen cities. Humana envisaged an $8 million loss on the project in building and promotional costs in its first year and healthy profits with time. Furthermore, Humana declared, if the "concept" caught on, the company planned to open a nationwide network of six hundred centers. Besides the $43 million for this project, Humana expected to invest capital expenditures of $200 million on other health care projects during the same period.

The effect of Humana's endeavors, if they prove successful, will be to change forever the manner in which Americans receive general medical care. No more going to the doctor's office; just about everyone in the country will line up at the drive-through window of a Humana MedFirst clinic.

Humana talks of "free-standing centers" to treat emergencies. But in a speech delivered before the American Hospital Association in Atlanta in October 1982, Charles Iobe, the company's vice-president of operations, Health Services Division, declared that none of Humana's forty-five presently open centers use the word "emergency" in their names. The Humana clinics, he went on, were essentially "primary care centers." "Some people have established MedFirst as their family physician." What Mr. Iobe failed to add was that the exclusion of the word "emergency" from the name of the clinics was an effort on the part of the company to conform with new laws. In the time between the planning and the inception of these clinics, many states had enacted laws that forbid the use of the word "emergency" in the title of any medical facility that does not remain open twenty-four hours a day, seven days a week, and does not possess all the necessary equipment for handling *real* emergencies on the premises.

It seems likely that Humana quickly calculated that its profits would be jeopardized if its free-standing "emergency" clinics were forced to be open all the time and as well always have on hand all sorts of expensive machinery. The company opted for a name change. Naturally, real emergencies will have to go elsewhere.

If you intend to open a chain of six hundred medical clinics you need doctors. Thus Humana bought Emergency Medical Services, a large group of emergency physicians, in early 1980. The same question that McDonald's asked a few years ago concerning the eating habits of America is now being asked by Humana concerning the health habits of the country. Are we, as a nation, ready for quick, medium-quality, medium-cost medical care? Are we ready for "fast-food" medicine? Humana is betting we are.

This company has outstanding 59,654,000 shares, of which 24 percent are closely held and 37 percent are owned by institutions. There are 27,800 shareholders of record. In 1982 Humana had a net income of $127 million on revenues of $1,516 million. Each share earned $2.14 as adjusted for a three-for-two stock split in January 1982. Earnings for 1983 were approximately $2.80 a share. The dividend on present shares has been raised 33 percent.

In September 1978 Humana doubled its scope through a merger with its large competitor, American Medicorp Inc. Currently, Humana operates ninety-one hospitals with 16,600 beds, and also its current forty-five MedFirst centers. Unlike some other companies in the field, Humana does not manage hospitals for others for a fee.

Thirty-four percent of Humana's revenues in 1981 were derived from Medicare and 5 percent from Medicaid, both government programs. The more hospitals Humana can buy, the more federal dollars will come its way. In May 1982 Humana acquired the Alaska Hospital and Medical Center in Anchorage, adding another 199 beds to its collection.

Medical economics being what it is, Humana may succeed with its drive-through concept of medical care. Suffice it to say that the company does have the resources to inflict the practice upon the public whether the public likes it or not. The $8 million loss Humana is willing to accept from initiating lower fees in its sixty-six centers over its first year of operation works out to approximately a $120,000 loss per center. You can be sure that the local G.P. could not sustain a $120,000 loss in one year and remain in practice.

But more important, neither the McDonald's hamburger nor the MedFirst health care can ever be truly first-rate. Few self-respecting physicians—likewise few self-respecting chefs—will accept work at the drive-through window; so the Tuesday special at half price will probably feature a somewhat less than topnotch clinician. Humana claims that it works in partnership with local physicians in the MedFirst centers; but in reality Humana employs these physicians, equips them, manages them, and in effect sets the whole show going.

Humana is not only a listed hospital chain owner; it also brought the concept of franchising to the health care field. For its MedFirst centers are first researched and then built by the company, which then franchises them to doctors. The initial losses are easily written off against the growing real estate depreciations. The MedFirst franchise operators then proceed to hire other physicians to work for them, and so they too soon enter the ranks of the entrepreneurs.

## HOSPITAL CORPORATION OF AMERICA

HCA of Nashville, Tennessee, is the world's largest hospital management company. Through an aggressive acquisition program begun in the late 1960s and a recent construction explosion, HCA now owns 172 acute care hospitals in the United States with a capacity of 27,689 beds. The company manages another 147 hospitals with 18,457 beds. Outside the United States HCA owns 16 hospitals with 1,640 beds and manages one hospital with 250 beds.

In this country HCA also owns twenty-five psychiatric hospitals with 2,841 beds. Its recent agreement to build a psychiatric facility for Vanderbilt Medical School has given it some prestige. However, its much-talked-of acquisition of McLean Hospital, the Harvard Medical School psychiatric hospital, fell through because of extreme opposition from the medical staff, who felt a teaching hospital should not be so closely tied to a for-profit corporation. In 1981 the company had a net income of $111 million on revenues of $2,064,064, 43 percent of which was derived from the Medicare and Medicaid programs. For 1982 the company's revenues were $3.5 billion.

The company has 58,112,000 shares outstanding; for 1981 it earned $2.23 per share. The 1983 figure is projected at about $3.80, up from $3.00 in 1982. Institutions, again mainly insurance companies, own 50 percent of HCA; many of these same insurance companies provide health insurance.

The facts and figures recounted here did catch the eye of the Federal Trade Commission. In August 1982 that body filed an administrative complaint against HCA, charging that HCA's acquisition of Hospital Affiliates International and Health Care Corporation could reduce free competition in the hospital field in certain areas of the country. HCA had purchased Health Care Corporation, owner of four hospitals, for 445,000 of HCA's shares in December 1981. Hospital Affiliates had been acquired by HCA from INA for $425 million cash and 5,390,000 shares. Hospital Affiliates had owned 157 hospitals and eighteen nursing homes before the takeover. At the time of the FTC complaint, HCA declared that it planned to dispute the charges, but to date the legal matter remains in limbo. Also in limbo is the question of how many hospital beds in the United States will eventually turn up in HCA hands. The company is the master monopoly player among the companies of the MIC; its appetite is voracious.

As of June 1982, HCA owned or managed a total of 50,994 hospital beds. With total revenues of $3.5 billion the figure comes to over $40,000 per hospital bed per year. Of this sum $2,160 was profit.

Why is it that a company like HCA can earn $2,160 profit per hospital bed per year while your local private hospital is sustaining a loss? The answer again lies in volume, quality, and inflated charges. Your local hospital, with perhaps 300 beds, is stuck with the surrounding population of patients and doctors. HCA has 50,994 beds to work with, so, if it loses a bit in Atlanta, it can make up the loss in Los Angeles. Chains play a balancing game; moreover, they have the time and the resources to try to "turn things around." HCA also has advertising dollars; it knows how to inundate an area with physicians in order to keep its hospital beds filled.

Unlike your local hospital, it appears to me that HCA and other companies of like persuasion are more prone to sacrifice quality and cut a few corners in order to turn a profit. For when Standard & Poor's reports HCA's yearly profits, the report ignores the fact that there were two fewer nurses this year than last in the intensive care unit.

Though it does not seem as flagrant a sacrificer of quality as National Medical Enterprises, HCA does not operate or strive to conduct a Mayo Clinic-type operation either. As a wheeler and dealer in the health care field, HCA is in a class by itself. The company owns substantial portions of other listed companies, companies that provide food, linens, machinery, and drugs to the hospitals HCA owns. The company also owns shares in other hospital companies, including, as we shall see, 20 percent of Beverly Enterprises, the largest owner of nursing homes in the country.

If one had to pick a single entity to exemplify the new entrepreneurial attitude in medicine, then HCA would surely serve the cause. Its formula of operation seems to be: Buy a hospital—or ten; cut corners on quality; buy a piece of the food and linen action; attract more doctors to the locality to fill the

116

beds; and, presto, turn a profit.

HCA's long-term goal seems to be not only to buy up more hospitals but also to acquire more shares in the companies of competitors, with a view ultimately to taking them over. Unlike McDonald's and Burger King, who seem content to fight each other, Hospital Corporation of America is attempting to buy everything in sight. Its philosophy appears to be, "Do not waste dollars to compete; use dollars to acquire."

Notwithstanding the FTC, HCA has direct ownership and management control over a tremendous number of hospital beds. When one adds the indirect control of stock ownership in other companies, one realizes to what extent giant corporations already control medical care standards in this country. How does a physician tell the cumulative owner of over 100,000 hospital beds the difference between medical right and medical wrong? You know the reaction you get when you try to give General Motors advice about the car they sold you.

The board of directors of HCA answers only to the company's 14,162 shareholders, and the only thing the shareholders want to see is a steady growth in profits. In the present medical economic environment it appears that the only possible way to keep increasing profits is to buy more hospitals and cut more corners on medical quality. To its credit, HCA has four physicians and one dentist on the eighteen-member board of directors. The numbers are unusual for such corporations, many of which have only a token M.D. on their board. Indeed HCA, as we've seen, was built from a single hospital, Park View Hospital in Nashville, by Dr. Thomas Frist, Sr., one of the great innovators in the industry. All the listed chains followed his methodology in building their own companies.

HCA is the twelfth-largest diversified service company in the country, ranked by sales, having moved up from nineteenth in 1981. The company employs 76,000 people, which is the third-largest number of employees of any service company in the land, behind only RCA and Halliburton.

## BEVERLY ENTERPRISES

Beverly Enterprises, thanks in no small part to the financial genius of Robert Van Tuyle and David Banks, is now the largest publicly held operator of skilled and intermediate health care facilities in the country. Van Tuyle and Beverly almost singlehandedly brought nursing homes out of the dark ages in the period of the last ten years. As of March 1982, Beverly, centered in Pasadena, California, operated 700 nursing homes, with 80,000 beds. As of March 1982, the company has issued twelve million shares, each of which earned $0.41 for the first quarter of 1982, a 39 percent increase over the previous year. There are now 5,600 shareholders of record, one of which is Hospital Corporation of America.

A close study of Beverly illustrates three crucial features that characterize the medical industrial firms. First, Beverly is strongly counting on the "graying" of America for its own growth. As the country's largest operator of nursing homes, Beverly has carefully studied census and actuarial figures and recognized the tremendous profit potential that exists in caring for the aged. America's population is slowly but inevitably changing from predominantly youthful to predominantly middle-aged. In 1970 there were 20,065,502 Americans age sixty-five and older, or 9.9 percent of the population. In 1980, the figures rose to 25,549,427 senior citizens, or 11.3 percent of the population. While the sixty-five and over population rose 27.3 percent in the past decade, the eighty-five-plus age group increased by 48.3 percent. In 1970, the median age of Americans was 28.1 years, while in 1980 it was 30.1 years. The change happens slowly, but as it occurs Beverly prospers. Hospital Corporation of America has also been inspired by the same analysis; they own 20 percent of Beverly Enterprises.

The second characteristic feature of Beverly is the speed with which it has grown. Founded in 1963, with three nursing homes and 245 beds, by Roy Christensen, a Mormon accountant from Utah, the company now operates 700 facilities with 80,000 beds. In the first quarter of 1982, the company acquired sixty-two more nursing homes. In that same quarter a new division, Heritage Health Care, was established to provide nursing home services to private patients. Again, in the same quarter, a 50 percent interest was acquired in Retirement Corporation of America, which manages a large retirement center in Florida; this division will serve as Beverly's exclusive developer of retirement centers in eighteen eastern states.

In early 1982, Beverly attempted to acquire Mediplex, which operates forty-two facilities with 4,750 beds; but in this case the Department of Justice challenged the acquisition on competitive grounds. Beverly is presently "restructuring" the acquisition to improve its palatability to the Justice Department. In July 1982, the company completed the acquisition of twenty-two nursing homes with 2,199 beds from Geri-Care Corporation of Minneapolis.

In 1980, Beverly increased its facilities by an astonishing 39 percent. In 1982, there was a further increase of 50 percent. Is it any wonder that Wall Street adores Beverly? Indeed, in 1980 you could have bought the stock for $7.50 a share; in November 1982, it was $39.00. For 1982, Beverly had revenues of $816 million, with net income at $26 million.

Since 1976 Beverly has increased revenues twelve-fold. Between 1981 and 1982 sales rose 68 percent while net income climbed by 62 percent. It is the second-fastest-growing company in the *Fortune* magazine listing of diversified service companies. Last year it ranked sixty-eighth by sales; two years ago it didn't even make the top 100 list.

The third standard characteristic of the company is the

interlacing of Beverly with several other companies of the MIC. As already mentioned, Hospital Corporation of America owns 20 percent of Beverly. In January 1982 the board of directors of Beverly elected Sam A. Brooks to be one of its members. It so happens that Mr. Brooks is senior vice-president of finance at HCA.

What is this cozy relationship between Beverly and HCA all about? To quote from Beverly's 1981 annual report:

*HCA's acute care hospitals offer us attractice nursing home develop-ment opportunities in nearby locations; a close working relationship with them will yield substantial benefits both to the elderly population and the company. The country's elderly will benefit from close physical proximity to nursing homes which, in many in-stances, offer a more appropriate level of convalescent care at far lower costs than available at acute care facilities.*

The quote is most remarkable for what it omits. What is going on is a close working relationship—including some common ownership—between the nation's largest operator of *acute* care facilities and the nation's largest operator of *chronic* care facilities. All that is lacking are funeral homes. You can be born in an HCA facility; have your tonsils and appendix removed there; give birth to your kids there; and when you get too old or run out of disposable parts, you can end up for the rest of your days in a Beverly nursing home. All the profits end up in the same pockets. When this mediglomerate does acquire funeral homes, it will be able to provide the proverbial cradle-to-grave care.

Not satisfied to bed down with HCA alone, Beverly is also flirting with the pharmaceutical giant Upjohn. In February 1982 Beverly and Upjohn Health Care Services, a subsidiary of the Upjohn Company, formed a joint venture corporation called Unified Home Health Care, Inc. The venture will "deliver in-home health care services." Patients who do not require the full-time services of a Beverly nursing home can now be cared for in their own residence. The institution that cares for the elderly will be owned in part by Upjohn, one of the largest manufacturers of drugs and pharmaceuticals in the world. It is a matter of record that the largest consumers of pharmaceuticals are the elderly. At the base of this tangled web is again volume. Beverly believes that, "Our size permits us to realize significant economics for all phases of nursing home operations—from the purchase of supplies to the training of more efficient personnel, to the lowering of overhead costs."

In fact, the Beverly-Hospital Corporation of America relationship seems to have been constructed to solve a vexing efficiency problem for the two health care giants. It is uneconomical to have a chronic care patient take up an acute care hospital bed. One thousand times a day some eighty-year-old grandfather is admitted to an acute care hospital because of a heart attack. Two weeks later when the worst is over, the family claims they can no longer care for Grandpa. Thus begins the expensive two-to-three-month search for a nursing home. While the search is on, Grandpa remains in the acute care hospital; most physicians will not kick Grandpa out, so he continues to receive expensive care. But now, if Grandpa ends up in a Hospital Corporation of America facility, he can easily be shunted to a Beverly nursing home. HCA achieves the opening of a valuable acute care bed and Beverly acquires a new customer.

The physically ill and elderly are not the only Beverly clients. In 1981 a new division, the Special Services Division, was formed to care for the mentally troubled, elderly, and the developmentally disabled. Beverly "expects this division to grow as more states turn to the private sector for help." Beverly must know, for, in 1981, a full 66 percent of the entire company's revenues was derived from federal and state funds.

Thus we see state, federal, county, university and private

hospitals going belly up, while highly profitable, listed hospital chains derive 66 percent of their revenues from taxpayer funds. The government is giving these corporations the money to grow, while at the same time, the Justice Department periodically questions the growth.

Beverly Enterprises, like other companies in the MIC, is a legally constituted corporation doing lawful business in the United States. However, it raises some thorny ethical questions. Is it correct for a pharmaceutical company like Upjohn to take its own cut in caring for the elderly, when these same elderly patients consume Upjohn's prescription drugs? Is it proper medical ethics for two large corporations with joint ownership and board members to own chains of both acute and chronic care hospitals?

What is legal in corporate law may be illegal or unethical in medicine. If a general practitioner examines you and then refers you to an orthopedist, it is illegal for that orthopedist to kick back a portion of his fee to the G.P. in consideration of the referral. Similarly a pharmacy cannot kick back a fee to a physician who writes a prescription that gets filled in the pharmacy. When an interconnected collection of corporate entities profits from acute care, chronic care, and pharmaceuticals, the lines of responsibility become rather blurred.

Yet the medical ethics are very clear. When a health professional refers a patient for further care, it is his duty and obligation to choose the best available under the circumstances, regardless of allegiances, personal preferences, or corporate connections. It does not matter whether we are considering orthopedists, physiotherapists, nursing homes, or pharmacies. The problems in corporate medical care are not necessarily restricted to honesty, ethics, or motives of individuals. The nature of a listed corporate entity is such that its prime motive for existence is the production of profit. Each individual in the corporation will advance or fall depending on the numbers he produces. It does not matter if he is packaging bottles in a pharmaceutical factory or administrating a hospital; he must produce profits. More often than not in health care the rendering of high-quality humane care is uneconomical. That is why so many of this country's hospitals are for sale.

Nevertheless, 1.3 million Americans, which represent 5 percent of those older than sixty-five, fill the country's 22,000 nursing homes. Total nursing home revenues this year will be $30 billion, and this sum is expected to double by 1990. Medicaid and Medicare programs pay half the Beverly as well as the national nursing home bill.

Despite its very bright outlook, Beverly is not without its share of problems. The company, though not involved in the tragic nursing home scandals of the early 1970s, recently had one of its patients die of accidental scalding. It has also received its share of health department violations.

Of equal concern, the AFL-CIO has made Beverly a priority target in its attempt to unionize health care workers across the country. At present 93 percent of the Beverly work force is nonunion, and the company, as one of the industry's leaders, is expecting a prolonged siege. The union claims that Beverly understaffs, underpays, and delivers substandard care for patients. Obviously this is a one-sided view, but it does indicate that future battle lines are taking shape.

In any event, Beverly intends to move aggressively forward. The company is constantly on the lookout for individually run nursing homes to buy. The small operators still represent approximately 40 percent of the industry. Beverly's plan calls for the purchase of 15,000 beds and the building of new facilities with a total of 2,500 beds every year for the next three years. Toward that goal Beverly announced in June 1983 an agreement in principle to acquire Beacon Hill America Inc., a concern that operates sixty-two nursing and intermediate care facilities with 6,908 beds in eleven states. The price of the acquisition was "well in excess of $50 million." To help fund the move, Beverly filed with the SEC a public offering of 1.2 million common shares. Hospital Corporation of America agreed to buy 680,000 shares directly from Beverly to prevent the new public offering from diluting its stake. The purchase is the one that raised HCA's stake in Beverly from 18 to 20 percent. For whatever it is worth, HCA has "agreed" not to acquire more than 25 percent of Beverly's common stock—all this after Beverly recently announced its proposed acquisition of CM Corporation of Sioux City, Iowa, and of Vilo Ocoiillo Inc. of Los Angeles.

October 1983 turned out to be a particularly rough month for Beverly. The company announced flat second-quarter earnings three days after (as mentioned earlier) the inspector general of the Department of Health and Human Services began to question the legality of Medicare paying a "return on equity" to home health care programs. Beverly stock fell seven points in a three-day period, a loss of 20 percent of value. Reports of third quarter earnings did nothing to boost stock value.

## CHARTER MEDICAL

Charter Medical is considered here in some detail not because of its size, but because, unlike many other companies, it at least has made the semblance of an effort to aspire to quality in medical care. The company owns twelve hospitals and manages thirteen others, mainly psychiatric, all with a total of 1,535 beds. In addition, Charter operates ten acute care and one specialty surgical center with a total of 1,643 beds. From corporate offices in Macon, Georgia, William A. Fickling, Jr., has carefully guided the company to carve out a special niche for itself in the psychiatric field.

The company has 8,117,645 shares outstanding, of which 20 percent are owned by institutions and 40 percent controlled by one member of the board—the latter making Charter a relatively closely held concern. For 1981 each share of the company earned about $2.30. Total revenues for 1981 were $228 million, of which 34 percent was derived from cost-based reimbursement programs at hospitals under Medicare, Medicaid, and Blue Cross plans. Net income for 1981 was $11.6 million. In 1982, revenues increased by 29 percent, giving the company another record year.

Other activities of the company include marketing of medical data services, providing financial consulting and development services to hospitals, and ownership and management of five medical office buildings. Charter employs over 4,000 people.

Unlike many of the other corporations, Charter allows its physicians some vote in matters of planning and policy. The board of directors of the corporation includes a practicing physician. The cover of the 1981 annual report features busts of Hippocrates, the Greek father of medicine, and Benjamin Rush, the father of American psychiatry. At the very least, one can say that the company knows something about the history of medicine.

The Charter Psychiatric Clinic in London has a distinguished reputation. Charter in fact was a cosponsor of the first World Conference on Alcoholism held in London, an admirable endeavor. The company has also recently formed a new Addictive Disease Division; addicting diseases are an expanding field of medicine. Charter has probably been able to maintain some semblance of professionalism because a single individual owns 40 percent of the company. It has largely avoided corporate entanglements except for some joint ventures in Saudi Arabia with Saudi Medical Services. In short, Charter has shown how a corporate entity can aspire to professional integrity by concentrating its activities in one medical field.

## AMERICAN SURGERY CENTERS

American Surgery Centers is a new wave company whose aim is to exploit the cost-containment factor in medicine and in minor surgical procedures. Some of the L. R. Singley success story I related earlier on; suffice it to say here that this Scottsdale, Arizona, company has displayed much imagination and a wealth of innovative ideas. A surgery center is a facility designed, equipped, and operated primarily for patients who require surgical procedures exceeding the capabilities of the doctor's office but not requiring hospitalization. The patient's own surgeon admits the patient and performs the surgery. Patients are discharged the same day, thus avoiding expensive hospitalization. It is estimated that 250 surgical procedures, or 40 percent of all hospital surgery, can be performed in a surgery center.

American Surgery Centers opened its first facility in Indianapolis, Indiana, in April 1982. Soon to open are newly constructed sites in St. Louis, Missouri, and Little Rock, Arkansas. Over the course of the next five years, the company expects to own and operate sixty such centers. American Surgery Centers International, a subsidiary of American Surgery Centers, is planning to open several centers in Mexico. In addition, in association with Bechtel International Corporation, the company is seeking a turnkey services contract; that is, a leasing contract that varies with use, at a value exceeding $240 million for three hospitals in the Middle East. As of August 26, 1983, the value of this potential contract to ASC remains questionable and controversial. (Several financial reporters have, in fact, questioned the accuracy of the company reports on the project.)

In a recent report, American Surgery Centers expressed its optimism about the future because of the philosophy espoused by the Reagan administration of cutting through "the clutter of governmental regulation." But again, the crux of the matter is getting only what you pay for. While it is certainly true that the surgical procedures performed in surgery centers are cheaper, procedure for procedure, than those performed in hospitals, there is no reliable  data available to indicate the comparative safety of the different operations. Wherever a general anaesthetic is administered, the risk of serious complication always exists, even if the surgical procedure is relatively minor. In a hospital one always has the backup of facilities and personnel—everything and everyone from an intensive care unit to on-site cardiologists and neurologists. Should a cardiac arrest or serious arrythmia occur in a surgical center, valuable time would be lost in getting the patient to the nearest hospital.

As of February 1982 the company issued 11,500,020 shares, of which 36 percent were owned or controlled by officers and directors, including 24 percent by one individual. There are a total of 3,500 shareholders. The company went public in September 1980; proceeds to the company were $1,686,370. At the time the shares were offered, the company owned only two items, an idea and a huge debt! Unlike companies such as Humana or Hospital Corporation of America, the jury is still out on whether American Surgery Centers will survive.

The ease with which the company raised over a million dollars by going public is testimony to the fact that the investment community loves a medical product. Cetus and Genentech realized this as well and had even more spectacular public offerings. Let us again remind ourselves that all three companies went public before they had anything to sell.

In 1981, American Surgery Centers had revenues of $0.10 million with a net loss of $0.10 million. In the first nine months of 1982 revenues advanced by 50 percent and the net loss widened to $709,924. During the course of the first six months of 1983 the price of the stock on the over-the-counter market advanced from $6 to $18 per share.

It will be a while before the final verdict is in as to whether surgery centers are effective cost-containment mechanisms. It will be necessary to determine if surgery center beds and procedures lead to a corresponding decrease—an economical and safe decrease—in the community hospital's inpatient beds and procedures.

## GENENTECH
## CETUS

Genentech and Cetus are the two Wall Street gene splicers that were the great compromisers of academic medicine but the darlings of the investment community. Armed with researchers who were enticed away from Stanford and the University of California with promises of stock and high salary, Genentech and Cetus are causing tremendous excitement on the stock market long before they have a product to sell.

Cetus was the first company in the field and remains today the most diversified concern dedicated solely to the development of commercial products through genetic engineering. The company was formed in 1971 by Ronald Cape and P. J. Farley and did most of its early work for a subsidiary of the Schering-Plough Corporation. In 1976 the company began doing substantial research for its own account. Even though most products or processes Cetus was pursuing were at preliminary stages, the company went public in March 1981 by offering five million shares at $23 per share. Before a product was even developed the company succeeded in raising more than $100 million; and until recently it is the interest on this money invested that provides a major source of income for the company. In June 1982 Standard Oil of California withdrew from a joint venture with Cetus concerning a new technology for manufacturing fructose, claiming that things were advancing a little too slowly for its satisfaction.

Though formed in 1976, Genentech beat Cetus to the punch by going public first in October 1980. The move caused a tremendous ripple on Wall Street. Genentech shot up from $35 to $89 on the first day of trading on the over-the-counter market, then gradually fell back to $35. The company has issued 8,048,834 shares, of which 20 percent is owned by Lubrizol Corporation, 10 percent by Wilmington Securities, and 4 percent by Flour Corporation. As well, the company has varying business relationships with Mitsubishi Chemical Industries Ltd., Corning Glass Works, Hoffmann-La Roche, and Monsanto.

Both Cetus and Genentech are responsible for having begun the medically questionable practice of reporting scientific findings first to the media, then to the professional journals.

The extent to which investors are willing to put their money into these ventures is symbolic of the lure of genetic engineering, but also of the power and influence of the MIC. Be it altered genes, nursing homes, or surgical centers, the attraction of medicine is magnetic, and the investment dollars keep flowing in. What is special about the little gene is that it proved the MIC could attract millions without anything to sell. It also showed that not only emergency physicians were ready to sell out research scientists were ready to join in as well.

In 1982 Cetus had revenues of $16 million with a net income of $3 million, much of which was derived from interest earned. Genentech in 1981 had revenues of $15.2 million with net income of $0.3 million. In 1982, revenues rose 41 percent but did not keep pace with expenses, and a net loss was sustained.

## HEALTH CARE FUND

Health Care Fund, guided by chairman and president Bruce G. Thompson, is a company that finances health care facilities. It has found a niche in the health industry that has proved very rewarding. For 1981 net income was close to $3 million, or $2.21 per share for the 2,295 shareholders of record. That net income represented an increase of 40 percent over the previous year on revenues, which had also risen 37 percent from $6.2 million to $8.5 million. The return on shareholders' equity was 18.9 percent in 1981, compared to 15.1 percent in 1977. For 1982 total income rose 16 percent and net income advanced 24 percent.

The company was formed in 1970 as a real estate trust to acquire and lease nursing homes and make nursing home construction loans in Ohio and contiguous states. The fund operates on a leveraged basis, thereby increasing its funds for investment. Its practice is to finance its long-term investments with proceeds from long-term borrowings and equity financings. The trust is managed by First Toledo Corporation, which was organized in 1971 for that sole purpose.

As of early 1982 the fund owned and leased forty-eight facilities with 4,206 beds to operators in Ohio, Indiana, Missouri, Pennsylvania, and West Virginia. About 66 percent of the beds were occupied by Medicaid patients receiving long-term medical care.

Health Care Fund presents an example of a private finance company in the medical industrial complex. Its customers are nursing home operators who have insufficient credit to borrow funds needed for construction. The fund essentially serves as a middleman between the large sources of capital such as banks and mortgage funds and the nursing home operators, regarded by these motivators as a poor risk.

Compared to such banking giants as Bank of America and Chase Manhattan, Health Care Fund is a small fish in a large pond. However, if more and more banks view hospitals and nursing homes as poor risks, Health Care Fund will prosper. Like Beverly Enterprises, it is also counting on the graying of America to spur the growth of the nursing home industry.

As with everything else, the insertion of a middleman increases the costs. The fund itself is exquisitely sensitive to current borrowing interest rates, and the recent Federal Reserve Board's tight money policies have slowed traditional flows of long-term mortgage financing to a trickle.

Consideration of Health Care Fund leads naturally to the topic of the accumulated debt of the entire health services industry. There is little doubt that the entire system is operating on borrowed time and money, and indeed an almost certain crisis is approaching. It is virtually impossible to accurately estimate the total accumulated debt of hospitals, nursing homes, and health care providers. Suffice it that the American banking industry estimates that 73 percent of independent private hospitals and nursing homes in the country are on the verge of defaulting on both long- and short-term outstanding loans. Close to 90 percent of county and state facilities operate in a perpetual state of default but are continually being bailed out by taxpayer funds. A recent study done by the Health and Human Services National Center for Heath Services Research determined that between one-fourth and one-third of the nation's voluntary hospitals can no longer generate sufficient revenues to cover expenses.

Banking institutions are understandably hesitant to force the debt issue with a local hospital or nursing home because not only does such an action constitute poor community relations, these institutions do not particularly want to become the owners of hospitals. However, as government pulls back the funding for health care, hospital debt will rapidly reach the point where bank creditors will be compelled to start closing down hospitals or selling them to one of the large mediglomerates. And though the financial reports of the chain hospitals look healthy now, further government cuts may even start affecting their debt structure and curtailing their ability to buy.

Certainly increasing debt in the short term will force many

hospitals and nursing homes into the corporate fold. In the long term the finances of the entire health care system look shaky. As a whole, the rapidly increasing debt of the health care system may make the staved-off default of Mexico, Brazil, and other countries seem relatively insignificant. We are dealing with 10 percent of the GNP, and the banks are understandably nervous.

The growth of a middleman financial company such as Health Care Fund is viewed by many investors and financial analysts as a danger signal to the entire health care field. The worry of the banks, coupled with the decreasing credit ratings of many health care providers such as hospitals and nursing homes, indicates the end of an era of rapid hospital growth in terms of building and renovating. The immediate choices for many small businesses will be either to sell to one of the MIC giants or to shut their doors permanently.

## BRISTOL-MYERS
## JOHNSON & JOHNSON

Bristol-Myers and Johnson & Johnson, companies that are household names, are two respected pillars of the Medical Industrial Complex. They do not own hospitals, doctors, or nursing homes; but they supply them and the public with drugs and general health care products. There is probably not a house in America where one could not find a product manufactured by one of these two giants.

For 1981 these two companies had total revenues of $8.9 billion (BM: $3.5 billion; J&J: $5.4 billion) and profits of $774 million (split roughly fifty-fifty). Both have a historical growth rate of about 13 percent and both take pride in their positions as leaders in a recession-proof business.

BM and J&J are but two examples of a long list of health care suppliers that are loved by investors because they grow at steady rates and supply the medical profession and public with essential items. Everything from Band-Aids to esoteric drugs comes from these or similar companies such as Upjohn, Merck, Eli Lilly, Foremost-McKesson (McKesson Corporation), Baxter Travenol, Fisher, G. D. Searle, and Pfizer.

Here are big companies with enormous assets. They supply essential products to the health field, and they have furnished this service for many years. However, in their search for profit and growth many of them are now getting involved in the health field as health providers—thus playing the corporate game of caring for and supplying materials to the same patients. We have seen, for example, how Upjohn joined with Beverly Enterprises. There are numerous other such alliances.

When Johnson & Johnson owns a piece of National Medical Enterprises, Bristol-Myers a piece of Hospital Corporation of America, and Upjohn a piece of Beverly, questions of medical ethics arise. Drug companies are supplying pills to hospitals they partially own. These drugs are prescribed by physicians whose salaries these hospitals pay directly or indirectly by contract. Of course the drug houses deny direct ownership of hospital chains, but a close inspection of their investment wing portfolios leaves nothing to the imagination. It is all legal, of course. But when you dig through the tangled web of subsidiaries and investments to find the intermingling of ownership and influence, you soon appreciate that it is the spirit if not the letter of the law that is being violated. And the truth is that drug houses would not have been so easily able to buy pieces of provider companies if those providers had not been listed on a stock exchange.

As the situation now stands, a drug house could conceivably buy enough shares on the open market of a large hospital chain to become a significant minority owner. The drug house would then own hospitals and the pharmacies within those hospitals. They would also be contracting with physicians who write the prescriptions. The fact is that on the stock exchange anything is possible. The bigger and more successful the hospital chain is, the more attractive an acquisition target it becomes. Any one of the major drug houses possesses the assets to buy and sell a hospital chain without batting an eye.

# IBM
# GENERAL ELECTRIC
# HEWLETT-PACKARD
# APPLE COMPUTER

Medicine is probably at least twenty years behind the fields of banking and technology in its use of computers. Nevertheless automated processes count for a great deal in most medical setups. IBM, Apple, General Electric, and Hewlett-Packard are examples of suppliers of expensive computers and technology to health care.

Expensive medical gadgetry is one of the prime reasons for escalating health care costs. The equipment is all so new and glittering that everyone feels they need it. IBM is a true Goliath among corporations, with 1981 revenues of $29 billion and profits of $3.3 billion. Eight percent of IBM's revenues and 6 percent of its profits are derived from medical sources, as are Hewlett-Packard's. Apple Computer, though much smaller than either IBM or HP, is making a concerted effort to sell home computers to the medical profession. General Electric is now the major manufacturer of the very costly CT scanner that every hospital feels it needs.

With so much money involved, it is easy to see why the suppliers of technology have a vested interest in the overutilization of the health care system. Rapid obsolescence—planned or unplanned—also plays a role here. No sooner is a medical machine bought than it is already out of date, and another required, probably at a greater cost. Medical people are notoriously poor judges of computer hardware and software and are consequently easy marks for the hard or soft sell. At any rate, just about everything that Silicon Valley has to offer has a taker in some hospital or other.

The result is that medical technology remains the costliest factor in the medical "business." Physician incomes pale to insignificance compared to the money spent on useless gadgetry. Hospitals will bargain with physicians and nurses over the cost of a box of Band-Aids and then go out and buy a million-dollar machine nobody knows how to use. Before they learn what one machine can do they are already ordering the next model. Hospital administrators love to scurry about the hallways with computer printouts dangling from their pockets, as if to say, "Here I am, modern man completely in control." Never mind that the hospital is deep in debt and patients are still dying of cancer. The printout seems to function as a security blanket for those who don't understand it.

The technology companies have provided the world with marvelous tools. The medical world has not yet learned their uses, but consumes them like bubble gum. The costs of the arrangement are enormous; indeed, it is virtually impossible to estimate the total bill for medical gadgetry. Hewlett-Packard derives 8 percent of its over $2.25 billion revenues from medical electronic equipment. When you consider that Hewlett-Packard is but one of hundreds of high-technology companies servicing medicine, you get some picture of the sums involved.

It is not only the hardware that is so expensive. HBO and Company sells and leases software systems to hospitals, clinics, and doctor offices. In 1982 it had revenues of close to $40 million, with profits close to $5 million. Software is much in demand. In 1982 Tymshare Inc., a New York–listed company, sold off its medical division to McAuto, which now sells the acquired software and computer time to hospitals.

# CARE CORPORATION

Care Corporation is a Grand Rapids, Michigan, company listed on the over-the-counter exchange. As chairman of the board, Robert W. Browne has his fingers in some unusual pies, including nursing homes, bowling alleys, tennis clubs, golf courses, real estate, and personnel agencies.

As of January 1983, Care owned and operated forty nursing homes with 5,243 licensed beds in six states. Through Care Personnel, Inc., the company also operates a health care personnel pool company. Through Concordia Corporation, of which Care owns 98 percent, it also operates ten bowling centers with 356 lanes, a tennis club, and a few golf courses. Through Care Real Estate Inc., Care operates a 112-unit retirement complex and an eleven-story, 135,000-square-foot office building. The company also owns 135 acres of vacant land.

In 1981, Care had net revenues of $65.4 million and a net income of $1.14 million for the 600 shareholders of the 2,194,828 shares. In 1981 health care activities accounted for 86 percent of revenues and 75 percent of profits, while recreation enterprises brought in 14 percent of revenues and 25 percent of profits. In the first six months of 1982 net income climbed 151 percent.

In January 1981, Care acquired Lifestyle Companies Inc., an operation of nineteen nursing homes. At this same time the company was involved in lengthy court and proxy fights in its effort to acquire Treadway Companies Inc., a company that runs bowling centers and motels. But shortly afterward Care gave up that attempt and sold its 484,189 shares in Treadway. In April 1981 Care acquired Redi-Nurse, Inc., a licensed home health care provider.

Care exemplifies the corporate need to acquire and grow,

without a concentration of interest in one field. The bottom-line profit figures are all that count, and if some are from bowling alleys and some from health care, then so be it. One can accept real estate ventures or retirement homes as related to health care; bowling alleys and nursing homes, however, make an odd combination. There are no physicians or nurses on the board of directors of Care Corporation; one suspects there may be several skillful bowlers.

Fully 73 percent of Care's revenues for 1981 were derived from the federal government's various Medicare and Medicaid programs.

## SEARS, ROEBUCK AND COMPANY

Sears is another household name. Nearly every shopping center in America has a Sears. This merchandising giant will shortly become an influential member of the Medical Industrial Complex. Sears owns Allstate Insurance, Caldwell Banker Real Estate, and Dean Witter Reynolds investment house. The company has as its goal to make universal "one-stop shopping" available in its stores—everything from soup to nuts to stocks and bonds and insurance. And it is only a matter of time before one will find a medical clinic as part of the Sears merchandise package.

As already mentioned, Humana intends to open in the near future six hundred free-standing primary care clinics. To facilitate such a large undertaking Sears already has everything in place. The company possesses ideal suburban sites with ample shopping center parking. It also has millions of credit card holders who could very easily, together with Sears employees, form the nucleus of a giant HMO. Sears' ownership of Allstate, one of the most important insurance companies in the country, will only make matters easier to implement.

The company fully appreciates the profit potential implied in the above analysis; indeed, it has been approached by a few chain hospital companies with a view to exploring the possibility of a health care partnership. Sears has also been approached by the large emergency room groups such as Spectrum, which would love to open some of its clinics in Sears stores. For the immediate future, though, Sears has decided to stay out of medicine, because the company fears it is too large a target for malpractice suits. The roadblock may only be a temporary one, however; and when it is set aside, Sears is almost certain to join the ranks as a major health provider.

## AMERICAN HOSPITAL SUPPLY

American Hospital Supply is the largest distributor of hospital and laboratory supplies in the land, and is rapidly becoming an important manufacturer of medical products. For the last twenty-five years this Evanston, Illinois, company has maintained a sterling growth record. Guided by its founder K. D. Bayes, the company manufacturers and distributes over 145,000 products used in the health care field.

The hospital division, which accounts for 57 percent of the company's sales and 59 percent of its profits, manufactures and distributes a variety of hospital supplies, including many disposable medical and surgical items. The laboratory division manufactures critical care and cardiovascular care materials, endoscopes, heart valves, blood-typing serums, specialty glassware, diagnostic reagents, and various instruments; it accounts for 27 percent of sales and 21 percent of profits.

There are 71,994,516 shares in the company, of which 59 percent are held by institutions. In 1982 each share earned $3.75, up from $3.08 in 1981. In 1982 the company had revenues of $3 billion and a net income of $229 million. Sales revenues for 1982 increased by 4.5 percent over those for 1981.

American Hospital Supply is a large company with a vested interest in systematic overutilization. Its sales and profits are pretty much directly proportional to the number of hospitalizations and the number of procedures carried out, both diagnostic and therapeutic. The company is also active in the general monopoly game so commonly played by the listed health care conglomerates. In March 1982 the company sold off its dental manufacturing operation to Sybron Corporation for $90 million. At the same time it announced that it was planning to invest $785 million over the next three years in its distribution network and in research development activities; of that amount, $225 million will go to product research, 73 percent more than during the prior three-year period.

AHS does not directly provide medical services, but its fortunes are closely linked to health suppliers such as Hospital Corporation of America, Humana, and National Medical Enterprises. The more patients these hospital owners can hospitalize and operate on, the more valuable the shares of American Hospital Supply become.

Ranked by sales, American Hospital Supply appears eleventh in the 1982 *Fortune* magazine listing of one hundred service companies. Net income in the second quarter of 1983 climbed 13.8 percent to $52.1 million, from $45.8 million in the corresponding quarter a year before. Second-quarter sales rose 11 percent to $814.3 million, from $733.8 million a year earlier. In July 1983 the company announced that it had signed a letter of intent to acquire Hoffmann-La Roche's Burdick & Jackson Laboratories subsidiary for an undisclosed price.

## AMERICAN MEDICAL BUILDINGS

The evolution of American Medical Buildings of Milwaukee has closely mirrored the changes in the American health care system over the last fifteen years. Essentially the company develops, designs, and supervises the construction and financing of medical buildings and clinics. Since its inception it has built more than three hundred structures in forty-four states. It is clearly furnishing a needed service in the current phase of health care restructuring.

American Medical Buildings has promoted the concept of a medical office building which is built and owned by a hospital in order to attract physicians to the area. A second successful idea and building is the ambulatory care center, in which hospitals provide outpatient X-ray, laboratory, and related services. A third concept of growing importance is the clinic building for group medical practices.

For a variety of reasons, American Medical Buildings expects to continue prospering in the present climate. The number of U.S. physicians is increasing proportionately much more rapidly than the general population, and physicians are consequently joining group practices in increasing numbers. The company is also relying on hospitals continuing to build more office buildings.

The company has issued 3,477,732 shares. In 1981 profits were $0.07 million on revenues of $15.9 million. Both revenues and profits were down from 1979 levels, due to the 1981 acquisition of the American Network division, which provides in-room entertainment service to hotels, motels, hospitals, and others. The transponder (a technical product) rights were purchased from Satcom IV, an RCA communications satellite. In addition to broadcasting motion pictures from 5 P.M. to 5 A.M., seven days a week, the American Network schedules and conducts live satellite teleconferences for hospitals, hotels, and motels. The company also broadcasts general-interest health care programs for hospital patients, and lectures, seminars and other programs for health care professionals.

# AMERICAN MEDICAL INTERNATIONAL

American Medical International, with corporate headquarters located in Beverly Hills, California, operates acute care and general hospitals in California, Texas, and the Sun Belt. The company owns or leases seventy-four hospitals in this country, possessing, in all, 9,713 licensed beds. During 1981 these units provided 2,113,396 patient days of care, up 32 percent from 1980. Fifty-two percent of revenues were derived from Medicare and Medicaid. AMI also manages an additional twenty-eight hospitals for other organizations.

In 1982, the company had a net income of $78.8 million or $2.30 per share (up 58 percent over 1981) on revenues of $1.1 billion (up 25 percent). Nevertheless the company looked for an even better performance in 1983 because of the addition of new hospitals, expanded services at existing facilities, and higher rates. It also expected increased utilization of existing facilities.

Besides running hospitals, AMI also provides respiratory therapy services, mobile CT scanning services, international health care consulting, and medical record and hospital management systems. The company also owns eight hospitals abroad, in England, Switzerland, and Australia, with a total of 854 beds.

AMI, like the other listed hospital chains, thrives on overutilization. The company has also shown itself to be a keen student of geography and demography. More than any other company in the field it has striven to follow the shifting American population from the Northeast to the Western and Sun Belt states, the desirable relocation regions for aging citizens. On a percentage basis AMI's performance on Wall Street has been one of the best.

In October 1983 AMI announced that it had signed a preliminary letter of agreement to sell seven of its acute care hospitals to Republic Health Corporation of Dallas for $45 million in cash. The seven hospitals constitute about 5 percent of AMI's total number of hospital beds. For Republic Health Corporation the acquisition would represent a considerable increase in its size, since at present the company owns only twenty hospitals. Prior to October 24, 1983, AMI was ranked forty-ninth in the Fortune 100 diversified service companies. It has thirty thousand employees.

On October 24, 1983, AMI merged with Lifemark in a $1 billion transaction, making the merged entity the second-largest owner of acute care beds in the country.

## AMERICAN STERILIZER

In my opinion American Sterilizer has thrived on the continued growth of the health care markets by institutionalizing for those markets the concept of planned obsolescence. From their offices in Erie, Pennsylvania, under the leadership of H. E. Fish, AS designs, manufactures, distributes, and services medical equipment, instruments, and related supplies. The thrust of the company's marketing approach seems to be to sell a hospital new cost-efficient equipment to replace the now "obsolete" equipment it sold the hospital two years before. And, as long as there is such overutilization in health care, AS will prosper handsomely.

The company's products include sterilizing, cleaning, and water-processing products; surgical support systems; and automated distributions systems. The Health-Care Disposable Product Division of the company sells a wide range of medical, surgical, and laboratory supplies, instruments, and equipment. Other products include hard and soft (AMSOF) contact lenses and air-powered surgical tools. There is hardly a hospital or clinic in the country that does not use products from American Sterilizer.

The company has issued 8,915,831 shares; for 1982 each share earned $1.40, up from $1.29 the previous year. In 1981 total revenues were $244 million, with profits of $11.5 million. The 1982 figures showed an 11 percent growth over the 1981 figures. Between 1972 and 1982 the company's revenues increased from $87 million to $244 million, a 300 percent increase. The steep rise closely parallels the steep rise of in-hospital bills over the same period.

## C. R. BARD

Over the last two decades America has acquired the habit of the disposable item—use once, discard, buy a new one—and medicine has acquired the habit too. Spurred on by high labor costs, the health care field has found that it is more economical to follow the country's trend to discard rather than to clean and reuse. The problem of course is that lately the costs of the disposable products have outstripped the labor costs, so that medicine now finds itself hooked on flashy, expensive, disposable products—long after the purpose has disappeared.

As medicine took the discard route, Bard of Muray Hill, New Jersey, made a fortune. The company produces and distributes disposable medical, surgical, diagnostic, and patient care devices; and it is the world's largest manufacturer of disposable urological products. Hospitals, physicians, and nursing homes account for 90 percent of Bard sales. Its surgical products category was formed in 1980 following the acquisition of Davol Inc., the maker of the Foley catheter. The Foley catheter became the foundation of Bard's urological products line, which now accounts for 32 percent of its sales.

In 1980 Bard also purchased Automated Screening Devices Inc., a manufacturer of automated, noninvasive microprocessor-controlled blood pressure monitors, for $5 million.

There are 9,856,614 shares of Bard, of which 12.5 percent is held by International Paper Company and 43 percent held by institutions. Earnings per share in 1981 were $2.20, up from $1.71 in 1980. In 1981, revenues were $330 million and net income was $22.5 million, the latter an astounding 46 percent increase over the previous year.

If *overutilization* is the buzzword for the companies of the medical industrial complex, it is the bible itself for a company that specializes in disposable products. More hospitalizations mean more procedures and the greater consumption of one-time-only products. Nor is it a coincidence that a paper company should own such a large chunk of a company so dependent on discardable products.

Many physicians will tell you that the quality of these disposable syringes, suture sets, and the like is poor, yet their cost now equals what the permanent instruments used to be. It is very difficult to perform any kind of intricate work with the plastic toys that are the order of the day, and yet hospitals persist in buying these expensive, attractively packaged goods.

In 1983 Omnicare Inc. announced that it had substantially agreed to buy all of the business assets of Bard's Inspiron respiratory division for more than $20 million. Round and round it goes—acquisitions and divestitures until nobody knows who is really putting the oxygen in your nose.

## BAXTER TRAVENOL

If one had to choose a listed company of the MIC for special commendation, it would be Baxter Travenol. Financially the company's record is outstanding; but so are its products and its services to the health care field.

Baxter Travenol is the country's leading producer of intravenous feeding solutions and manufacturer of kidney dialysis equipment. The experience of the Second World War and the

Korean War taught medicine the tremendous importance of intravenous infusions in sustaining life; and the company's products in the field have kept pace with the latest medical developments. Countless thousands of lives have been saved by the use of its intravenous solutions.

Unlike almost all other supply companies, Baxter Travenol has always been willing to produce "orphan" solutions; that is, medically necessary drugs that are used in such small quantities as to be unprofitable to produce. The company has also always been very responsive to the requirements of the medical profession in furnishing it with drugs that have very limited uses.

Revenues for 1981 were $1.5 billion with profits of $151 million. The company has issued 70,945,453 shares, of which institutions own 65 percent. In 1981 sales increased by 123 percent over the preceding year, and each share earned a hefty $4.15, up from $3.72 in 1980.

In keeping with its tradition of high quality, Baxter Travenol received FDA approval to market a superb plastic blood-collection-and-storage container, which will substantially simplify collection and transfusion procedures. The company's kidney dialysis equipment and supplies are as good as the state of the art permits; and there is also strong demand for its continuous ambulatory peritoneal dialysis machines, which allow kidney patients freedom of movement. The company has profited from overutilization but, unlike so many other companies, it has not skimped on quality.

What sets Baxter Travenol apart from so many other companies is its professional attitude. It takes its responsibility as a supplier of essential items to the medical field seriously. Its production costs are concentrated on quality control and not on packaging and marketing, which often consumes 20 to 40 percent of a manufacturer's costs. It is a rare company indeed.

# BEECHAM GROUP

How would you like to own shares in a company that manufactures both penicillin and Seven-Up? Beecham, a predominantly British company that is also listed in the U.S. over-the-counter market, is such a company. Beecham Group is a leading British producer of pharmaceuticals for medical and veterinary use, animal health products, and animal feed additives and chemicals. Prescription medicines include semisynthetic penicillins, allergy vaccines, vitamin products, gastrointestinal medicines, and others. During 1981 the company introduced Augmentin, a new broad-spectrum antibiotic that is supposed to be effective against more bacterial infections than any other oral penicillin or cephalosporin.

Besides penicillin, the company also markets Brylcreem, MacLean's and Aqua-Fresh toothpastes, Sucrets, and Vitabath. Recent acquisitions include Bovril food products and Jovan Inc. perfumes. In 1977 Beecham acquired the Calgon division of Merck & Company. And in April 1982 the company reached a franchise agreement under which it would manufacture and market Seven-Up in Great Britain. Here then is a listed company that markets hair cream, toothpaste, dog food, perfume, soda pop—and penicillin. In my opinion, a company with so many diverse investments clearly has no special commitment to medicine.

The company's breadth of activities has certainly been rewarded. Total sales for 1982 increased 18 percent above those for 1981, and during the same period profits climbed 31 percent. Pharmaceuticals contributed 51.6 percent of profits, while consumer products contributed 48.4 percent.

In terms of U.S. markets Beecham is no giant, but the variety of its products and the ubiquity of its market make the company a true member of the mediglomeration. North and South America contributed 24 percent of its total profits, the

United Kingdom contributed 37 percent, the remainder of Europe 25 percent, and Asia and Australia 16 percent.

## BIOCHEM INTERNATIONAL

Biochem International is an example of a growing high-technology company that has prospered with the explosion in utilization of operating rooms and intensive care units. It began work in 1978 when it acquired some of the patents and technology associated with the blood gas chemistry business of General Electric's Medical Systems Business Division. The company designs, manufactures, and sells medical systems that instantly and continuously monitor blood gases, electrolytes, and pressures. As complicated surgical procedures such as heart bypass and organ transplants become more common, such equipment becomes widely needed for postoperative care.

In 1982 the company's revenues were $5.34 million, with losses of $0.64 million. For 1982 there was a healthy 36 percent increase in revenues but a profit loss due to vendor supply problems. The company issued 2,060,830 shares of common stock, of which officers and directors own 36 percent.

Biochem International is an example of how in health care, whenever a technological advance is made, some company somewhere realizes substantial spinoff profits. Part of the horrendous bill you receive after a stay in an intensive care unit of a hospital is due to the cost of expensive equipment such as the sensor devices manufactured by Biochem International. Indeed the profit makers are everywhere in health care delivery: for BI, which manufactures the device; for the hospital, which "sells" you the device; and for the two or three middemen who are usually involved in such transactions as well. You also pay the costs of advertising and packaging.

When you have your heart bypass operation other companies besides Biochem International profit. First there is the

147

hospital itself: Hospital Corporation of America made $2,000 profit per hospital bed last year. A computer company such as IBM profits from the registration procedure. Then there are the blood tests from Biochem International, the X-rays from General Electric or Picker, and the hospital food and linens from ARA Services. Then there are the surgical instruments from American Hospital Supply or American Sterilizer, the disposable goodies from Bard, and the intravenous solutions from Baxter Travenol. While you are comatose in the operating room and the intensive care unit, there are the sensing devices from Biochem International and the gases from Air Liquid. Then of course there are the multitude of dressings and gauzes from Johnson & Johnson.

If there are complications, you will need the kidney dialysis equipment from Baxter Travenol and numerous electrocardiograms from Hewlett-Packard. If you are lucky enough to survive, a bed at Beverly Enterprises awaits your convalescence. Indeed, it is estimated that a typical hospital admission that involves major surgery benefits no less than forty-six listed U.S. corporations. Is it any wonder then that you must virtually mortgage your life away in order to rid yourself of a few gallstones or a blocked coronary artery?

The new equipment is life-saving and for that reason entirely admirable. We are living longer because of many medical technological breakthroughs, and who would begrudge the inventors and manufacturers of the new devices a monetary reward for their efforts? But perhaps they are asking too much and their equipment is being overutilized.

## COLLAGEN CORPORATION

Collagen Corporation is an example of a company that had a relatively easy time raising capital because of the virtually assured profits ahead. Collagen manufactures biomedical products used to replace or repair lost or damaged human

148

tissue. The company's only major product is Zyderm Collagen Implant (ZCI), which is a solution of purified collagen packaged in a syringe. It is used to treat soft-tissue contour deficiencies resulting from age, trauma, disease, or surgery. In some cases the untested material has been used for voluntary, some would say unnecessary, operations such as face-lifts, and the results have not always been free of complications.

In July 1981 the FDA granted Collagen approval to market ZCI as a medical device rather than as a drug. What the FDA was thinking about at the time is difficult to understand. The product is a *drug;* one would be hard pressed to explain how a solution that comes in a syringe can be classified as a *device.* Needless to say, the classification of "device" is very beneficial to the company, because unapproved drugs are much harder to market than unapproved devices. In addition, manufacturers of devices are allowed to recoup research and development costs during clinical investigations.

In October 1981, three months after FDA approval was granted to ZCI, the company went public with an initial offering that raised $13.5 million. The company has issued 4,767,896 shares, of which Monsanto Company owns approximately 24 percent. Besides the relationship with Monsanto, Collagen has granted Schering-Plough the exclusive right to market ZCI outside the United States, Canada, and Japan.

Before ZCI appeared on the market, the company in 1981 had revenues of $1.97 million with a loss of $1.2 million. In 1982, with shipments of ZCI going out, revenues went up 400 percent, and for the first time a profit was made. In 1982 the company's revenues were $7.4 million and net income was $0.70 million.

## HBO & COMPANY

HBO is a leader in the exploding hospital information systems industry. In general the health care industry has had the

149

reputation of being behind the times in its use of computers; HBO has been making a serious attempt to eliminate the lag. As of 1982 the company has installed 307 systems at 254 hospitals in thirty-nine states. Essentially the firm offers proprietary software and computer hardware made by others for the processing of patient, department, and financial information.

HBO's Medpro system processes patient and departmental information. Its Ifas system processes the financial and billing information. Its Clinpro system processes separate departmental information. All three systems are sold on a turnkey basis, at a leasing rate that varies with use, and are compiled in modules, so they can be assembled in different ways to meet specific needs.

HBO, in my opinion, has capitalized on hospital administrators' lack of knowledge about computer systems by providing mediocre systems at high prices. The only computer services that a hospital really needs—basic financial, billing, and accounting operations—could be purchased relatively inexpensively from any service company. The flashy HBO systems appear to be redundant, break down often, and serve little real purpose in terms of patient care; and they certainly add little to a hospital's efforts to achieve some degree of cost containment.

The company has 7,228,679 common shares. For 1982 revenues were $38.9 million, with profits of $4.97 million. In December 1981 HBO acquired Medical Data Corporation for 212,219 of its common shares.

## HUNTINGTON HEALTH SERVICES

Huntington Health Services operates four general hospitals with a total of 681 beds, four extended-care facilities with a total of 345 beds, and three facilities with 379 beds for the developmentally disabled. About 46 percent of the general care patients are on Medicare, and 86 percent of the chronic patients are on Medicare and Medicaid.

The company has issued 2,065,047 common shares and for 1982 revenues were 66.7 million. In August 1980, Blue Cross of Southern California, the fiscal intermediary for the Medicare program, charged that Huntington had overbilled Medicare the amount of $400,000 between 1976 and 1979.

When a physician overcharges Medicare and is found out, the deed is called fraud; the physician usually loses his license, pays a fine, and may even go to jail, When a listed corporation overcharges Medicare and is found out, the deed just calls for an "audit adjustment": the money simply gets paid back. It is bad enough when taxpayer dollars end up as excessive profits in the pockets of health company shareholders; it is certainly worse when these companies are involved in overcharging the public and the penalty is just an ineffectual slap on the wrist.

Huntington Health Services is an example of why the Department of Health and Human Services must begin taking close look at chain hospitals. The SEC, the FTC, and the Justice Department are mainly corporate regulators. What is vitally needed is an overseeing agency that understands the practice of medicine and that has the teeth necessary to force listed health care providers to comply with the moral and ethical demands of the field.

## LONG'S DRUG STORES

Long's Drug Stores operates 164 super drug stores located mainly in California. Drug items account for 19 percent of sales; food and beverages, 23 percent; housewares, 17 percent; cosmetics and toiletries, 13 percent; tobacco, magazines, sporting goods, toys, and stationery, 13 percent; photo finishing, 6 percent; and other, 9 percent.

Long's prescription drugs are usually advertised at very low prices—they are often loss leaders. Super drug chains now fill 69 percent of the nation's prescriptions, and 86 percent of the people who enter the store buy, besides a prescription drug, at least one other item.

In 1981, revenues for Long's Drug Stores were $1.0 billion, with profits of $30.3 million. The company has issued 10,567,490 shares, of which the Long family controls 31 percent and institutions hold 31 percent.

The outlook for the drug chains is extremely bright. As America ages, the consumption of prescription drugs increases proportionally. Because of security problems and high costs, more and more corner drug stores will cease operations in the coming years, and the chains will as a consequence increase their market share.

Chains such as Long's have had a great deal to do with the decrease in the retail price of prescription drugs. The drugs are still expensive, but they would certainly cost even more if the chains did not use them as loss leaders. The public is the obvious beneficiary of this chain operation strategy.

## NATIONAL MEDICAL CARE

As of March 1982 National Medical Care was operating 160 outpatient artificial kidney treatment centers, 37 obesity control clinics, and 2 pilot clinics for diabetes treatment. Through a subsidiary, Erika, Inc., the company manufactures and distributes dialysis supplies and equipment to patients on home treatment and to hospitals and other dialysis centers. The Med-Tech subsidiary distributes respiratory therapy supplies to hospitals, doctors, and home patients.

In 1981 National Medical Care had a net income of $19.7 million on revenues of $285 million. Eighty-one percent of revenues and 83 percent of profits were derived from health care services, while sales of medical suppplies contributed 19 percent of revenues and 17 percent of profits. There are over eighteen million shares, 37 percent of which are held by institutions. There are approximately fourteen thousand shareholders of record. The 1982 revenues advanced 3.8 percent, but net income declined 18 percent due to rising operating costs. The company has been negatively affected by Medicare cutbacks in reimbursement for outpatient dialysis treatments.

National Medical Care's dialysis centers represent the participation of the corporate entrepreneur in a treatment previously restricted to hospitals. The services these centers provide are nevertheless necessary and laudable. Still, there is a danger involved in detaching sophisticated medical procedures from a hospital setting. Three deaths that recently occurred at one Dallas center is a case in point. The *Wall Street Journal* reported that a malfunction in dialysis equipment (manufactured, by the way, by Extracorporeal Inc., a subsidiary of Johnson & Johnson) caused fluid to overheat, resulting in cardiac arrest and sudden death for three patients. While any equipment can malfunction, in a hospital setting such machinery is routinely checked on a daily basis and patients are carefully monitored throughout the procedure. More careful attention to both equipment and patient plus the backup services of a hospital might possibly have averted this tragedy. In 1981, 8,000 chronic kidney failure patients received 1,472,000 dialysis treatments in National Medical Care facilities. This represented a 15 percent increase over the previous year. Eighty percent of the charges up to $138 per treatment (excluding the physician's fee) are covered by Medicare.

The future of this company is closely linked to Medicare. If cutbacks in reimbursements are severe the company will suffer and profits will continue to decline. National Medical Care can in a sense be considered a bellwether operation because, more than most other proprietary health care suppliers, its fortunes are closely linked to the funds made available by federal programs.

## BIOTECH CAPITAL CORPORATION

Biotech Capital Corporation is a second-generation offspring of the MIC. The company produces no goods or materials itself and supplies no direct services to health care. It is rather an investment company that invests in different private and public high-technology medical companies. It supplies money to new concerns and achieves an equity position in the company.

Currently Biotech holds significant positions of ownership in Associated Biomedic Systems, American Cytogenetics, and Clinical Sciences. American Cytogenetics is involved in the cancer detection screening of microscopic slides; Clinical Sciences manufactures diagnostic reagents and equipment for clinical laboratories, food processing, and veterinary testing.

Biotech has a total capitalization of $16.1 million, with 3.5 million shares outstanding. This type of company has a direct stake, albeit a comparatively small one, in the success of the MIC's selling sophisticated high-technology items to the health care system. More specifically it prospers directly from the overutilization of laboratory facilities.

## FOREMOST-McKESSON

Foremost-McKesson (McKesson Inc.) is involved in a wide variety of activities and services, including drugs and health care products, food, wine, and industrial chemicals. In 1981 the company had net sales of $4.4 billion and net income of $68.6 million. Of the more than sixteen million company shares 47 percent are owned by institutions. The health care group accounts for 42 percent of FM's revenues and 29 percent of its profits. The division includes the only national distribu-

154

tor of ethical (prescription) and proprietary (over-the-counter) drugs, toiletries, and sundries, serving retail as well as hospital pharmacies. The wine and spirits group accounts for 19 percent of revenues and net income and is the largest wholesale distributor of wine and spirits in the United States. The chemical group is the largest independent full-line distributor of chemicals in the United States. It accounts for 14 percent of revenues and 13 percent of profits.

The foods group recently announced an agreement to sell its Foremost Dairies division for $65 million. The company also announced in June 1983 that it had signed a letter of intent to acquire Zee Medical Products, a company that installs and stocks industrial first-aid cabinets and distributes safety products.

With the sale of the Foremost dairy group, the name of the entire company changed to McKesson Corporation as of July 1983. The firm presents an example of the unusual diversification that corporate practices often lead to—different and disparate products made and peddled by the same concern, with an inevitable blurring of priorities.

## BLUE CROSS

Eighty million Americans carry a Blue Cross card and, as the Blue Cross advertisement continues, $0.93 of every subscribed dollar is returned to members in benefits. Blue Cross is a group of seventy-five independent nonprofit corporations and, as such, the agglomerate cannot truly be considered part of the MIC. However, the company plays a major role in underwriting health care in this country and so must be considered in any study of health care delivery systems.

Blue Cross writes the checks for the health care of close to one-third the nation's population. The organization is one of the prime forces behind the recent drive for cost containment.

155

With so many subscribers miscalculations can be disastrous. In 1981 Blue Cross of Northern California, for example, underestimated the rise in health costs and went heavily into the red. In 1982 the company hiked its subscriber rates, but the raise may still fall short of the 11 percent medical inflation for the year.

Each Blue Cross organization operates independently, with its own officers and board of directors. In some states the organization works closely with Blue Shield; in others the two systems are entirely separate. Occasionally mergers between two different offices take place in order to achieve greater efficiency, such as the recent joining of Blue Cross of Northern and Southern California to form Blue Cross of California.

Blue Cross sells individual health policies and group policies mainly through employers. Recently the company entered the HMO market, with "take care" type programs. Blue Cross does not face much competition with its individual policies, but in group policies the field is very competitive. Many private profit companies sell life insurance to groups, and these companies often throw in health insurance at a cheaper rate when they make a sale. In order to meet the market Blue Cross itself took the unusual step recently of offering life insurance in limited regions.

Together with government, Blue Cross is a major force in the attempt to initiate programs to reduce health care costs. The organization has powerful lobbies at the state and federal levels of government that are constantly exerting pressure of one sort or another for government to act in ways that meet its demands.

Each Blue Cross office is a little bureaucratic unit in itself, employing claims processors, data entry people, financial analysts, and medical economists. More than anything else in the office there are mountains and mountains of paper. For every subscriber visit to a physician at least ten pieces of paper are generated; when a hospitalization is involved the paperwork triples.

The technocrats who work for Blue Cross view physicians as the adversary. They believe the physicians order too many tests and X-rays and hospitalize too many patients needlessly for too long a period. The physicians bill Blue Cross and try to squeeze out every nickel of their fees; Blue Cross on the other hand tries in every way to minimize the reimbursements. To hear Blue Cross tell it, the physicians are bankrupting the system. Never does one hear from its salespersons that a mere 2 percent of the health dollar goes to physicians. The really large payouts Blue Cross makes are to hospitals. As it happens, Blue Cross initially was very enthusiastic about the chain hospitals of the MIC, but the bills remained as high or higher than before, causing the company to reconsider.

One of the great contributions that Blue Cross has made in the last few years was to finally drum home to everyone the idea that there was a limit to the number of health care dollars available and that somehow a system had to be developed to effect a more efficient distribution of exhaustible resources. The disservice the company performed was to point a finger at physicians as the cost-causing culprits and exclude them from any cooperative planning effort.

Using the "prudent buyer" concept, Blue Cross will soon begin pre-negotiating fee schedules with physicians and hospitals for its subscribers. Since the medical field is now very competitive, the new system will ultimately mean lower reimbursement for doctors and hospitals. The chain hospitals believe that the new system will also put many independent hospitals out of business, and thus make more hospitals available for them to buy at bargain prices. Even if this is correct, the system will also inevitably cut deeply into the profitability of the corporate hospitals themselves regardless of how efficient they become.

But whatever happens, most observers agree that the country can no longer afford the kind of medical care to which it has become accustomed. The question that physicians are posing is whether one can entrust the changes that must come to the Blue Cross technocrats just because that company happens to insure so many Americans. Just like government, Blue Cross is notorious for working outside the usual medical channels. Rather than deal with medical staffs, it negotiates with hospital administrators. It avoids county, state, and national medical societies and chooses instead to bargain in the offices of government legislators and bureaucrats.

With Blue Cross insuring the health of 80 million Americans and government insuring another 43 million, the country can be said to already have a makeshift national health system. If and when a truly universal program is legislated, it will obviously have to work with or through Blue Cross. Blue Cross is in essence a partial monopoly.

Blue Cross states that Americans have cast their ballots (with money) for their policies. In point of fact most subscribers have little choice. The vast majority of them are covered under group policies taken at the workplace; and, in the field of individual policies, there is precious little competition in most areas of the country.

The tortuousness of the logic Blue Cross and hospital associations use to accuse physicians of fiscal irresponsibility can best be seen in the December 1982 pamphlet prepared by Arthur Young & Company, "Briefing on Health Care." Commenting on Blue Cross's announcement of its prudent buyer plan, the booklet declared:

*The new program is designed to reduce health care costs by offering subscribers financial incentives to obtain health services from preferred providers that have contracted with the plan.*

But soon after the appearance of the booklet a spokesman for the California Hospital Association stated:

*The Blue Cross program will aggravate hospitals' financial strains because [other] private insurance companies will be negotiating contracts to avoid shifting unmet costs to private patients.*

(The shifting of costs to patients who can afford to pay because they are privately insured is a practice that hospitals have traditionally adopted in order to balance the books.) And now the *pièce de résistance*. The hospital association spokesman added:

*The program will be frustrating for hospitals because physicians— not hospitals—determine the volume and type of service used.*

The thrust of these remarks is that it is physicians who over-utilize the system and force Blue Cross to become a prudent buyer and hospitals to be squeezed. But in the same month Seton Medical Center, a member hospital of the same California Hospital Association mentioned above, began a series of advertisements on KCBS radio in San Francisco that literally pleaded with MediCal patients to visit the hospital. MediCal patients are essentially nonpaying customers, whose health care is underwritten by the State of California.

In the midst of all this talk by Blue Cross, government, and hospital associations of *physician* overutilization, one sees *hospitals* advertising in the media. On the one hand they are screaming about overutilization and on the other they are pleading with the public to pay them a visit. When hospitals beseech the public to come on in, they are essentially advertising their most available, expensive, and overutilized area, the emergency room.

When hospital associations respond to Blue Cross by pointing the finger at physicians, one might legitimately inquire why so many of them are tripping over themselves to attract more physicians to their areas. In fact, hospitals love overutilization and actively encourage it. Through all of this, physicians have little to say on the matter.

The Blue Cross organizations across the country have really served the public quite well and are asking reasonable questions. The answers they are preparing are inadequate; and their total avoidance of physician input is regrettable. They are, in a sense, biased. They realize that the times have put great power in their hands and they appear to be out to "get" the doctors and hospitals they view as adversaries. For better or worse, the people who insure the health of eighty million Americans are finally having their say. But that may have come too late, even for Blue Cross.

It is now generally recognized that what is desperately needed in this country are preventive health programs. It is estimated that every dollar spent in preventive care can save $1,000 in curative care. The vast majority of diseases that afflict Americans are for the most part preventable or avoidable. Conditions such as obesity, atherosclerosis, hypertension, and alcoholism are preventable with sound care, exercise programs, diet, etc. Blue Cross now has the numbers and the power to do something about these problems, yet the thrust of all their energies is focused on the curative side. Instead of squeezing the fat from their subscribers, they are squeezing doctors and hospitals. So long as Americans continue to eat too much, drink too much, and exercise too little, the bills on the desk of Blue Cross will continue to grow. You lower medical costs by preventing illness, not by holding back reimbursements for the cure.

The main goal of Blue Cross is to survive in this difficult atmosphere. There are 1,800 life and health insurers in the United States today, and it is estimated that by 1990 only 400 will have survived. In 1981 Blue Cross of Northern California saw an increase over the previous year of 24.5 percent in claims expense. During that year it paid out more in benefits than it received in premium income, and only investment income allowed the company to close near the break-even point, with an excess of $330,000.

Blue Cross of Northern California, serving only northern California's population of ten million, paid out $2.7 million in claims each working day of the year, or $352,000 each hour. The blueprint for survival includes pushing for preadmission hospital testing, elimination of many routine admission tests not ordered by physicians, copayments and deductibles, coordination of benefits, and benefit designs for less costly outpatient services.

Looking at Blue Cross as an example of all the others, one can see that the organization simply cannot go on indefinitely paying out $1.6 billion per year on six million claims and still retain subscribers who can afford premiums. The entire system is close to the breaking point; and if Blue Cross cannot manage, probably no such system can.

## KAISER FOUNDATION HEALTH PLAN
## KAISER FOUNDATION HOSPITALS
## KAISER-PERMANENTE MEDICAL GROUPS

Kaiser-Permanente's reputation as the manager of the most successful prepaid health care plan in the country is deserved. There are a multitude of reasons, many of which occurred by chance, why its practice of prepaid medicine through a health maintenance organization has worked so well. The plan was initiated by Edgar Kaiser, son of the founder of Kaiser Industries, back in the 1930s. He arranged with Dr. Sidney Garfield, a surgeon who had been practicing in the Mojave Desert, to care for workers laboring on the Grand Coulee Dam on a prearranged daily fee per worker. The plan was later enlarged, with the recruitment of other physicians, to cover Kaiser Shipyard workers in San Francisco during World War II. After

161

the war the prepaid plan was offered to the community at large. Since then the organization has grown to become the largest group health insurer in California; it has 4.1 million subscribers nationwide, which represents 37 percent of all HMO subscribers in the country. Kaiser is the second largest operator by revenues ($2.4 billion in 1982) of multifacility systems in the country. Besides California the system operates in Oregon, Hawaii, Maryland, Virginia, and Washington, D.C.

Kaiser owns hospitals and contracts with physicians, who work their way, after a few years, into full partnership in the organization. Each hospital functions with its own administrators and committees, but there are central committees that make overall decisions. The physicians play a large role on all committees and share in the profits at the end of the year.

The Kaiser Foundation Health Plan is a nonprofit organization. It is not connected to the Kaiser industrial empire. The Health Plan contracts with and pays the nonprofit Kaiser Foundation hospitals. It also contracts with and pays the Kaiser-Permanente Medical Groups, which consist of 4,500 physicians, nurses, and nonmedical personnel, and which operate for profit. In 1982 the Kaiser Foundation Health Plan, having received $2.4 billion in revenues from its 4.1 million subscribers, paid the foundation's 28 hospitals, 107 outpatient centers, one nursing facility, and one psychiatric center a total of $1.09 billion. It also allocated $1.18 billion to the Permanente Medical Group. A full $170 million was spent on administration, community services, and retained earnings.

In the Kaiser system everyone has a vested interest in cost containment: the company itself, the physicians, and the subscribers. There is a direct relationship between cost containment and both physician profits and subscriber fees; for, since the premiums are prepaid, all concerned want to keep the subscriber out of the hospital.

When a subscriber joins Kaiser, he or she is assigned to a Kaiser facility, a hospital or clinic.In cases of dire emergency, or where Kaiser does not offer a particular service, the patient goes elsewhere and Kaiser still pays. Since Kaiser physicians practice only in Kaiser-owned facilities, they control access to the system by the subscriber; the arrangement has a direct effect on hospital and facility utilization.

The Kaiser physician has a vested interest in keeping Kaiser subscribers healthy and out of the hospital; at the end of the year a formula divides the organization's profits among them. The system works because a closed circle is involved. In other types of plans neither the hospitals nor the physicians are exclusively committed, so there is very little control of utilization.

Because it owns its own facilities, Kaiser realizes substantial savings by centralizing departments and expensive equipment. In the San Francisco Bay Area, there are Kaiser hospitals in San Francisco, South San Francisco, Oakland, and Redwood City, yet only the Redwood City facility has a CT scanner and full-fledged neurosurgical services.

Similarly, expensive cardiac surgery is centralized so that not every facility has universal capability. In some cases Kaiser has found it cheaper to contract with outside facilities for certain services rather than run those services themselves. Thus, for example, on the San Francisco peninsula, Kaiser pediatric cancer patients receive radiation therapy at University of California hospitals. Unlike the medical community at large, Kaiser has realized that not every facility requires every new piece of expensive gadgetry, and that not every facility needs every specialty represented.

The subscriber receives a good financial package. There are, however, two main problems which Kaiser has always had. First, the variability of service. Patients often do not have a single physician for themselves: on one visit their child may

163

be examined by one pediatrician, while on a second visit one month later their child may be seen by a different pediatrician in the same clinic. Kaiser tries to minimize this variability whenever and wherever possible, but the problem remains widespread. Second, the quality issue has always plagued Kaiser. In the 1960s and early 1970s the average income of Kaiser physicians was substantially lower than that of physicians in private practice in the same community. Thus Kaiser employed numerous foreign-trained physicians and other physicians who, for one reason or another, could not make it in private practice. In the mid-1970s things began to change. The average incomes of private practice physicians fell and those of Kaiser physicians rose. The costs and hassles of running a private practice were becoming prohibitive, and, suddenly, working for Kaiser began to look very attractice to many doctors. No office rent to pay and no insurance forms to fill out. But most of all the job offered a steady income with very few nights or weekends on call. Kaiser quality is now considered to be on par with any hospital, except perhaps the university hospitals.

Whereas most physicians make errors of commission—that is, they do too much—Kaiser physicians are generally inclined to make errors of omission—that is, they do too little. If you bump your head and go to a hospital emergency room, you are much more likely to have your skull unnecessarily X-rayed at a private hospital than at Kaiser. You are also much more likely to be admitted to a private hospital for observation regarding any condition than you are if you showed up at a Kaiser facility. The private hospital has a vested interest in doing X-rays and admitting patients, while Kaiser profits if it can legitimately avoid the tests and admissions. Because of this system, one occasionally reads about a huge lawsuit being brought against Kaiser for having missed something. Kaiser is a large target and lawyers love large targets. When you sue

Kaiser, you not only sue a physician and a hospital but an entire multihospital health plan. In California, where legal suits are virtually a universal pastime, Kaiser hospitals have legal judgments rendered against them at a rate similar to that against any other hospital. But comparisons are difficult to make, because most of Kaiser's medico-legal disputes go to arbitration by prior consent of patients.

Despite Kaiser's success, it will be very difficult for other organizations to emulate its example. Kaiser began gradually and built hospitals at a time when doing so was affordable. Also their mode of operation is opposite that of the MIC companies, which profit by overutilization. Thus one cannot imagine a Hospital Corporation of America starting a Kaiser-like system unless the overall rules of the game change. The only outfit that may make an attempt to start similar HMOs is the INA–Connecticut General–CIGNA conglomerate. That organization has vast resources and is already in the insurance business. It owns both hospitals and prepaid plans, and it does try to operate its plans according to Kaiser's underutilization model. The company has yet to deal with the centralization aspect of the model, and it has yet to show that it can work comfortably with physicians running the medical show. If Kaiser were a corporate entity, it would clearly be a natural target for a takeover by CIGNA, and I believe this is still a reasonable possibility. CIGNA has all the money and Kaiser-Permanente has all the experience and medical know-how.

Kaiser is the only organization in the country that has successfully competed with Blue Cross on a large scale. In California, Blue Cross is outstripped by Kaiser in group plans, and continues to lose groups to Kaiser at an increasing rate. Kaiser rates are lower; also Kaiser can control its costs, while Blue Cross is at the mercy of every physician and hospital. In California, Blue Cross, as already mentioned, is now attempting to pre-negotiate rates with physicians and hospitals. But in my opinion it will never succeed in competing with Kaiser, because it is subject to an open-ended system, whereas Kaiser operates in closed loops. In order for any prepaid system to succeed it must own the hospitals and have a vested interest in underutilization. Kaiser has shown that with these factors one can deliver quality care at reasonable rates—at least rates more reasonable than prevail in the surrounding community. Until Blue Cross can actually control hospitals it will not remain a stable system.

Kaiser and the MIC employ opposing methodologies. Kaiser underutilizes for profit, the MIC overutilizes for profit. The gestalt of the times is working in Kaiser's favor. As government payments shrink, more hospital beds will remain empty. Empty Kaiser beds mean profit for Kaiser, while empty Humana beds mean losses.

In order to survive, the MIC companies will have to stop buying hospitals and start buying prepaid HMO plans or initiating them on their own. It is however far easier and more profitable to grow as Kaiser did—by building facilities to accommodate increasing subscribers. The MIC will have to work out plans to accommodate an excess of facilities, a far more difficult task if your primary profit mechanism has been overutilization. In a real sense Hospital Corporation of America will be closing the barn door only after having redecorated the barn.

Why is it, then, that the corporations of the MIC raced to buy hospitals instead of prepaid plans? Why did it choose the overutilization method rather than the opposite? The answer lies in corporate image and is the precise reason many investors believe in listed companies. Corporate image is based on growth. Bigger is always better, and the faster you get bigger the better. It would be extremely difficult for a corporation to boast about empty hospital beds. Annual reports look better when you can say that this year the company owns 200 hospitals, whereas last year it owned only 100; shareholders love the fact that this year the company admitted a million patients, whereas last year it admitted only half a million. It is numbers that sell stocks. The more hospitals you own and the more hospital beds you control, the better you look to people accustomed to judging production lines.

It is even an acceptable and successful corporation strategy for a company to inform its shareholders that this year profits were down because the company bought ten new hospitals. As long as something gets bigger, the company is perceived as growing. The cardinal sin of corporate life is stagnation. Even a growing company is at risk if its rate of growth slows down.

If Humana ever reported a significant decrease in admissions the stock would tumble in an hour. If the stock were indeed to fall the members of the board of directors and the officers of the company would lose a fortune, because much of their remuneration lies in stock and stock options. In such a situation heads would roll, all the way down the chain of command. Thus everyone in the company has a life-and-death vested interest in more hospitals, more beds, more admissions, and more lab tests.

So long as a hospital is owned by a listed entity overutilization is essential to oil the Wall Street wheels. Underutilization is so foreign to corporate thinking that prepaid medicine seems an improbability—except to those insurance companies like CIGNA and INA that understand profit by prepayment.

As America gets older the mediglomerates claim that utilization will increase. Nobody doubts that fact. But where will the money come from? The problems of Social Security are only the tip of the iceberg for the elderly. There is no guarantee that government resources will ever equal the costs of their care and keep. Buying hospitals now in order to run them at a profit to serve the elderly seems to me a monumental gamble. Yet that is the long-range policy of the MIC.

# SOME COMPANIES OF THE MIC

| COMPANY | PRODUCT | STOCK EXCHANGE | 1982 SALES REVENUES (MILLIONS) | SYMBOL |
|---|---|---|---|---|
| ADAC Laboratories | Medical diagnostic imaging | NASDAQ | 22.9 | ADAC |
| ARA Services | Linens, food, physicians, nursing homes | New York | 2,916.0 | ARA |
| Acme United Corporation | Medical instruments | American | 40.4 | ACU |
| Affiliated Hospital Products, Inc. | Surgical gloves | American | 52.0 | AFH |
| Alo-Scherer Healthcare | Topical medication | NASDAQ | 10.0 | ALOE |
| Alza Corporation | Drug-release systems | Pacific | 4.6 | AZA |
| American Diagnostics | Diagnostic kits | NASDAQ | 2.5 | ADGN |
| American Hospital Supply | Hospital products | New York | 3,000.0 | AHS |
| American Medical Buildings | Medical buildings | American | 15.9 | A |
| *American Medical International | Chain hospitals | New York | 914.0 | AMI |
| American Medi-Dent, Inc. | Contract dentists & facilities | NASDAQ | 1.4 | AMDT |
| American Sterilizer | Hospital equipment | New York | 244.0 | ASZ |

| Company | Business | Value | Exchange | Symbol |
|---|---|---|---|---|
| American Surgery Centers | Surgery centers | 0.1 | NASDAQ | SRGY |
| American Vision Centers | Franchise retail outlets | 7.0 | NASDAQ | AMVC |
| Bard (C. R.) | Medical, surgical devices | 330.0 | New York | BCR |
| Bausch & Lomb, Inc. | Optical goods & instruments | 533.0 | New York | BOL |
| Baxter Travenol | Intravenous-feeding solutions | 1,504.0 | New York | BAX |
| Becton, Dickinson and Company | Hospital supplies | 1,066.0 | New York | BDX |
| Beecham Group | Pharmaceuticals & consumer products | 2,511.0 | NASDAQ | BHAMY |
| Benedict Nuclear Pharmacy, Inc. | Radiopharmaceuticals | 0.9 | NASDAQ | BENE |
| Berkeley Bio-Medical, Inc. | Nursing homes and hospitals | 3,841.0 | Pacific | BBM |
| Beverly Enterprises | Nursing homes | 816.0 | New York | BEV |
| Bio Logicals, Inc. | DNA, RNA instrumentation | 2.8 | NASDAQ | BIOLF |
| Bio-Medicus, Inc. | Medical devices | 0.6 | NASDAQ | BIOM |
| Biochem International | Blood-measuring devices | 5.7 | NASDAQ | BIOC |

| COMPANY | PRODUCT | STOCK EXCHANGE | 1982 SALES REVENUES (MILLIONS) | SYMBOL |
|---|---|---|---|---|
| Biotech Capital Corporation | High-tech medical investments | NASDAQ | 0.5 | BITC |
| Bristol-Myers | Pharmaceuticals and consumer goods | New York | 3,496.0 | BMY |
| Care Centers, Inc. | Nursing homes | NASDAQ | 15.0 | CCEN |
| Care Corporation | Convalescent and rehabilitation centers, bowling alleys | NASDAQ | 91.0 | CARC |
| Cetus Corporation | Genetic engineering | NASDAQ | 9.8 | CTUS |
| Charter Medical | Chain hospitals | American | 294.12 | CMD |
| Collagen Corporation | Biomedical products | NASDAQ | 1.9 | CGEN |
| Community Psychiatric Centers | Psychiatric hospitals | New York | 90.0 | CMY |
| Concept, Inc. | Disposable medical products | NASDAQ | 16.1 | CCPT |
| †Connecticut General Insurance | Insurance HMOs | New York | See CIGNA | CGN |
| Damon Corporation | Medical and laboratory services | New York | 146.0 | DMN |

| Datascope Corporation | Electronic medical instruments | NASDAQ | 31.2 | DSCP |
|---|---|---|---|---|
| Del Laboratories | Drugs, cosmetics, toiletries | American | 63.0 | DLI |
| Delmed, Inc. | Disposable plastic medical products | American | 40.6 | DMD |
| Diagnostic Products | Immunodiagnostic test kits | NASDAQ | 9.4 | DPCZ |
| Dow Chemical Company | Chemicals, ethical pharmaceuticals | New York | 11,873.0 | DOW |
| Ealing Corporation | Life-science equipment | NASDAQ | 11.7 | EALG |
| Eastman Kodak Company | Photographic, X-ray producers | New York | 10,337.0 | EK |
| Electromedics, Inc. | Temperature systems | NASDAQ | 3.8 | ELMO |
| Foremost-McKesson | Drugs, health care products, food | New York | 4,493.0 | FOR |
| Genentech | Genentech engineering | NASDAQ | 15.2 | GENE |
| General Electric | Electrical products, CT scanner | New York | 27,240.0 | GE |
| HBO & Company | Hospital information systems | NASDAQ | 38.9 | HBOC |
| Hazleton Laboratories | Biological research | NASDAQ | 53.1 | HLAB |

| COMPANY | PRODUCT | STOCK EXCHANGE | 1982 SALES REVENUES (MILLIONS) | SYMBOL |
|---|---|---|---|---|
| Health Care Fund | Nursing homes | NASDAQ | 8.5 | HCFDS |
| Healthdyne, Inc. | Electronic medical equipment | NASDAQ | 16.5 | HDYN |
| Hewlett-Packard | Computers | New York | 3,578.0 | HWP |
| Hospital Corporation of America | Hospital chain | New York | 2,064.0 | HCA |
| Humana, Inc. | Hospital chain | New York | 1,924.0 | HUM |
| Huntington Health Services | Hospital chain | American | 46.0 | HHS |
| Hybritech | Monoclonal antibody products | NASDAQ | 0.36 | HYBR |
| ICN Pharmaceuticals | Drugs | New York | 49.0 | ICN |
| IMMutron | Immunodiagnostic equipment | NASDAQ | 0.17 | IMMU |
| †INA Corporation | HMOs | New York | See CIGNA | INA |
| INA Investment Securities | | New York | See CIGNA | IIS |
| International Business Machines | Computers | New York | 29,070.0 | IBM |
| Johnson & Johnson | Health care products | New York | 5,399.0 | JNJ |
| Laser Industries | Surgical laser systems | American | 5.20 | LAS |

172

| Company | Description | Exchange | | Symbol |
|---|---|---|---|---|
| ‡Lifemark Corporation | Chain hospitals | New York | 273.0 | LMK |
| Lilly (Eli) | Drugs | New York | 2,772.0 | LLY |
| Long's Drug Stores | Chain drug supermarket | New York | 1,005.0 | LDG |
| Marian Laboratories | Drugs and hospital products | New York | 118.6 | MKC |
| Merck & Company | Drugs | New York | 2,929.0 | MRK |
| National Medical Care | Artificial kidney centers | New York | 285.0 | NMD |
| National Medical Enterprises | Hospital chain | New York | 894.0 | NME |
| Neo-Bionics | Antibodies, enzymes for diagnosis and therapy | NASDAQ | 0.0 | NEOB |
| Pfizer, Inc. | Drugs | New York | 3,250.0 | PFE |
| Scherer (RP) Corporation | Encapsulation products | NASDAQ | 170.0 | SCHC |
| Scientific Leasing, Inc. | Leasing scientific and medical equipment | American | 3.8 | SG |
| Searle (G. D.) | Drugs | New York | 942.0 | SRL |
| Sears, Roebuck | Retail chain | New York | 27,357.0 | S |
| Squibb Corporation | Drugs | New York | 1,524.0 | SQB |
| Sterling Drug, Inc. | Drugs | New York | 1,793.0 | STY |
| Stryker Corporation | Hospital equipment | NASDAQ | 42.9 | STRY |

| COMPANY | PRODUCT | STOCK EXCHANGE | 1982 SALES REVENUES (MILLIONS) | SYMBOL |
|---|---|---|---|---|
| Sybron Corporation | Health products | New York | 647.0 | SYB |
| Syntex Corporation | Specialty pharmaceutical | New York | 711.0 | SYN |
| Temp-Stick Corporation | Scale systems | NASDAQ | 1.3 | TEMP |
| Teva Pharmaceuticals Ltd. | Pharmaceuticals | NASDAQ | 68.7 | TEVIV |
| Thompson Medical | Health care products | New York | 83.9 | TM |
| Tyco Laboratories | Electromedical equipment | New York | 552.0 | TYC |
| United Medical Corporation | Cardiovascular products and care centers | American | 7.5 | UM |
| Vari-Care, Inc. | Health care services | NASDAQ | 18.1 | VCRE |
| Whitman Medical Corporation | Health care products | NASDAW | 0.2 | WHIT |

*Prior to October 1983 merger with Lifemark Corporation.

†On March 31, 1982, INA and Connecticut General merged to form CIGNA. For 1982, revenues were $11.7 billion.

‡Prior to October 1983 merger with American Medical International.

## 1981–1982

| LISTED COMPANY | HEALTH FACILITIES OWNED OR MANAGED | HOSPITAL BEDS OWNED OR MANAGED |
|---|---|---|
| *American Medical International | 74 | 9,713 |
| Beverly Enterprises | 591 | 80,000 |
| Care Corporation | 39 | 5,243 |
| Charter Medical | 36 | 3,178 |
| Hospital Corporation of America | 362 | 50,994 |
| Humana, Inc. | 91 | 16,600 |
| Huntington Health Services | 12 | 1,525 |
| †Lifemark Corporation | 35 | 4,563 |
| National Health Enterprises | 65 | 9,207 |
| National Medical Enterprises | 212 | 26,176 |
| | 1,517 | 207,199 |

*Prior to October 1983 merger with Lifemark Corporation.

†Prior to October 1983 merger with American Medical International.

# 9
# AN UNSUITABLE MARRIAGE

If hospitals and doctors don't work together, they'll destroy
each other.

—ENZO DiGIACOMO
Vice-President for Medical Affairs
Mercy Hospital, Springfield
Massachusetts (1983)

Despite the fact that I have used the term freely throughout this
book, there really is no such thing as a United States health
care "system." There are physicians, hospitals, insurance
plans, and government entitlement programs. Labeling these
chaotic mechanisms a "system" is inaccurate, to say the least.
A system implies predictability; however, if a person faints on
some street corner in America, I defy anyone to predict where
that patient will end up and who will pay the bills.

Just as the health care system is a fantasy, the corporation is
a fiction. A corporation is simply a group of people producing
goods or services under clearly defined legal structures; it is in
reality a "people umbrella." Corporations do not do things;
people do. Corporations are not taking over health care; the

177

people who work within corporations are. Stating that wide-spread corporate involvement in health care is bad for us simply means that the wrong type of people are exerting a great measure of control over the nation's health. The laws and economics of corporate life mold the employee to behave in a manner that will advance his career and at the same time advance the common interests of his fellows. Corporate life is a team sport with decision by committee. Increasing corporate involvement in health care means, in human terms, that the gray flannel suit is replacing the white coat.

Moreover, there is no "crisis" in medical care. The professional level of care delivered in this country is the highest quality available on earth. Many doctors do earn a large sum of money but this has absolutely nothing to do with the nation's high medical bills. In 1984 if every physician provided all professional services free of charge it would only cut total health care spending by less than 4 percent. Less money was spent in 1981 for physician services than for hospital toilet paper, tissues, and other assorted paper products. For every dollar that Medicare spends on physician fees, it spends $3 on bureaucratic salaries and $98 on hospital and nursing home charges. While in 1981 the average physician had a gross income of $93,000, that income derived from only $2 of every $10 billed to patients. In no other profession or business venture does the bottom-line provider get to keep so little.

Medical costs are increasing. Health care programs and facilities are going broke. And many people have strong emotional feelings about physicians. All this does not a crisis make. The real crisis is still a few years away. It will occur if the U.S. mediglomerates achieve a monopoly position and completely take over American health care.

It is estimated that fully 11 percent of community hospitals and 66 percent of nursing home beds in this country are now controlled directly or indirectly by listed corporations. It is conceivable that by the end of the decade a handful of corporations will control 25 percent of hospital beds. The Justice Department notwithstanding, we are beginning to see a monopoly in health care services. The recent merger of Lifemark and AMI adds further credence to this view. It will soon become virtually impossible for any small organization to compete. Even the university hospitals will be in jeopardy.

Health care now makes up 10 percent of the gross national product; by 1990 the figure will be closer to 16 percent. Simple arithmetic reveals that by the end of the decade the mediglomerates will be capturing close to 4 percent of the GNP. The MIC sees a $118 billion pot of gold at the end of the rainbow. Despite all government actions this figure is expected to continue increasing, especially as America shifts from a young to a middle-aged population.

We are now on the verge of a major shakeup in the industry. In the next five years the shrinking health care dollar will bring all the sellers into the market. There will be an abundance of hospitals for sale. More and more beds will end up in the corporate column. The independent community hospital is on the verge of following the family farm and corner grocery into extinction. The companies of the MIC will become more closely interwoven. Already, as we have seen, some of the relationships are very disturbing. Johnson & Johnson, for example, is involved in animal health, diagnostic imaging products, nuclear medicine, ultrasound, digital X-ray, and CT scanning as well as everyday pharmaceuticals. The company finds itself also at the forefront of technology, with new nuclear magnetic resonance scanners.

As if these were not enough, Johnson & Johnson also owns a dialysis business, a critical care company, and an intraocular lens business. It also sells Vascor heart valves. With so much to sell the medical world, is it any wonder that the president of Hospital Corporation of America was elected to the board of Johnson & Johnson?

The true giants of the MIC are the insurance companies such as CIGNA and pharmaceutical companies such as Johnson & Johnson. Any one of them could buy and sell a Humana or Hospital Corporation of America in an afternoon, and the danger is they may just do it. Certainly with officers of the company in common they may already be thinking in these terms. If so, we will soon be looking at a situation in which manufacturers, distributors, and prescribers of the drugs are one and the same entity. The seeds of the problem have been planted in fertile corporate soil and only a strict sort of ethical and legal control over the activities of the mediglomerates can ward off the collapse of the health care system that is otherwise sure to come.

As matters now stand, two eventualities could upset the Wall Street applecart and one seems almost inevitable. If the health care economic squeeze gets too tight, the chain hospitals will see cuts in profitability; and because they are so large, they could tumble quickly. A change in physician attitude, if it develops, could also spell disaster for the conglomerates.

Physicians, by and large, admit patients to the local hospital no matter who owns it. Recently, however, the first rumbles of conscience from the medical community have begun to be heard. Articles have started to appear expressing the moral dilemma: on the one hand, physicians are striving for cost containment, but on the other, they are practicing in hospitals having a vested interest in overutilization. Most physicians still remember their medical school professors whose brilliant clinical acumen and impeccable ethics set the standard for the conduct of a medical practice.

But many physicians quickly sacrifice the ideal for the

money. They opt for a nice office and buy a nice house in a nice suburb. They meet nice friends and join nice clubs. Instead of working at dark and drab inner-city hospitals, which they did as residents, they now work in sparkling new steel-and-glass Humana or NME facilities.

But the best medicine is practiced with, and in full view of, the questioning eyes of medical students, interns, and residents, without regard to costs or computer printouts. The danger of medical monopoly is not so much that it will maintain high prices; the tenor of the times is against that, but that it will control the system that is responsible for providing one of the fundamental rights of life—the best health care society can offer. The inescapable fact is that corporations are concerned only with questions asked by their shareholders. Time and again we have witnessed corporate plant closings and factory relocations for profit reasons without the slightest regard to community needs. Who will stop Humana from closing an unprofitable hospital in a community that has come to depend on it? And who among its stockholders has the knowledge or the interest to question why or how an operation was performed?

That doctors recognize the moral problems involved in working for a corporation is a necessary first step toward reforming the system. But the overall out-of-control element in the American health care system is its dollar cost—a cost so high that without significant changes it might bring the entire system, chaotic as it is, crashing down upon us.

The dollars are just not there anymore. The costs of delivering health care are escalating, while government and other third-party payers are all negotiating their payouts downward. And the MIC, monopoly or not, is going to begin to see a drop in its profits.

The census of the nation's emergency rooms showed that occupancy was down 12 percent for the last quarter of 1982.

For the same quarter the average hospital bed occupancy was down 9 percent. Employers, employees, and health insurers are all beginning to realize that underutilization is in their interest. The fact that Blue Cross of Northern California in 1981 lost money on its insurance operation is tremendously significant. The organization cannot afford to make the same mistake twice.

Employers and insurers are raising the deductibles, while governments are eliminating many beneficiaries from their rosters. A new classification known as MIA, or "medically indigent adult," has been established; where previously the state and federal governments picked up their tab regardless of where they were treated, MIAs will now be compelled to seek treatment in county facilities only.

While it is true that our population is shifting south and west, and America is growing older, I believe it is inevitable that fewer new hospitals will be needed, because of a changing pattern in utilization. Just as Americans turned to small foreign cars and energy conservation, they will soon realize the benefits of less utilization of the health care system. Recently, the federal government estimated that in 1980, 80 percent of emergency room visits were not necessary and 40 percent of hospitalizations were not medically indicated. It concluded that Americans could do just as well in health care with one-third the present number of hospital beds.

Already some employers have informed their employees that annual dollar-for-dollar savings on health care will be remitted to them: Utilize the health system less and receive back the consequent savings at year's end. Employees are in effect being told to stay away from doctors as much as possible and avoid unnecessary lab tests, X-rays, and hospitalizations. The most recent Aluminum Workers Union contract adds new medical deductibles workers must pay, but gives each worker $700 yearly to pay these charges. Employees may choose among different health insurance options and may keep what they don't spend.

In the past, medical work, in a variation of Parkinson's Law, expanded to fill the time doctors had available and the beds hospitals had available. But in the very near future, I believe medical work will shrink as the money supply shrinks. The less money Blue Cross and government indicate they have, the fewer gallbladders will be taken out. I don't care how old Americans become or how many move to the Sun Belt; there will be relatively fewer overall hospitalizations in this country in 1985 compared with 1982 and there will be proportionally far fewer in 1990 compared with 1985. Americans are not going to be very happy about it, but they were not delighted to wait in gasoline lines either. All the same, they learned their lesson well. They consumed 18 percent less gasoline in 1981 than they did in 1980.

No serious student of the issues believes that America can continue paying the madly escalating medical bills that it paid in the past—in fact it has already started to put the lid on in various ways. Now whether prospective patients subscribe either to voluntary efforts, positive incentive experiments, incentives mixed with controls, or mandated government regulations, most analysts agree that a further decline in hospital utilization will ensue. In terms of their viability, the chain hospitals will find themselves in the same position the airline companies did, but the pressures in their case will be coming from the opposite direction. The airlines were nearly annihilated by deregulation; the hospitals will suffer from more regulation.

Government can use hospital budget ceilings or so-called CAPS, price-setting, certificates of need, and various other monetary techniques to force its will upon hospitals. Government also regulates licensing. Besides, 50 percent of hospital income comes from government third-party payments such as

Medicare, Medicaid, and others. The Social Security acts and the National Health Planning and Resources Act mean that hospitals can lose government assistance when they do not comply with its directives.

In the near future the government dollars will shrink and regulations will begin to cut the fat from the hospital system, signaling the end of the kind of overutilization that filled many unnecessary beds. There is just no way that profits can continue to grow in such a climate. Sometime in mid-1985 we can expect a sharp decrease in chain hospital profits.

I do think, however, that the future will be kinder to companies that have a product or service that stresses cost containment or efficiency. When third-party payments decrease there will be a need for health care services delivered outside the hospital setting. Thus companies running free-standing clinics or surgical centers where an overnight stay is not called for will be in an advantageous position.

In order to cut costs, physicians will have to decrease the number of X-rays, laboratory tests, and hospitalizations they order. To accomplish this, they will have to become more familiar with their patients' records, probably through the use of computerized medical charts. Such retrieval systems have been developed by some companies and the field offers potential for profit for those so inclined.

The first insurance companies that offer incentives to their policyholders *not* to utilize the system may also harvest good profits in the coming years. Increasing the deductibles has not proven a successful means of accomplishing this goal. What is needed is something like a partial return of the premium to those clients who remain healthy. The private carriers are gradually realizing that the vicious cycle of increased health costs followed by increased premiums does not serve their best interests.

Companies in the nursing home field will also grow in the

near future. The census figures indicate that more beds will be needed for the elderly in the future. Under the new prospective payment rules Medicare implemented October 1, 1983, nursing homes and convalescent facilities (for short-term care) will become very important. Hospitals will receive only a limited sum for the Medicare sick based on diagnosis and will therefore have to discharge patients earlier to some other facility. They will have to develop working relationships with nursing homes and convalescent facilities. What is true for Medicare patients today will be true for the entire population in the next few years.

At the moment, in terms of profit, the future seems brightest for the provider-insurer conglomerates, while the pharmaceutical companies and genetic engineering firms will continue to grow. However, without controls and significant changes in the system, the health field will remain rampant with technical controversy, stock hype, and misinformation while providing mediocre medical care at inflated costs, all inevitable by-products when medicine and monopoly mix together.

# 10
# TOWARD A
# WORKABLE
# FUTURE

What you are seeing is the structural basis for a national health
system without any legislative basis.
                            —JEFFREY FIELDLER
                              AFL-CIO


I certainly do not have the magic solution to the medical
dilemmas facing this country in the next ten years. But I
believe we must strive *now* for gradual, reasonable, adjustment
that takes full cognizance of the trends, forces, and institutions
that have been evolving over the last twenty years. Most people
agree on a need for cost containment but everyone waves the
flag from a different side of the fence. Every serious proposal
for a cost-effective system is preceded by an orgy of finger
pointing at who is perceived to be the villain. Some blame
government while others blame the medical profession. Many
castigate insurance companies, patients themselves, and even
the media. Whoever and whatever is to blame, it is clear that
the American people are now more eager to accept any changes
in the system that will lead to a decrease in costs.

In pursuit of this elusive goal, various groups have produced their own mechanism of change, much of it open to question. The federal government believes you can trim costs by restricting the Medicaid rolls, increasing the deductibles and copayments for Medicare, and narrowing the services for which Medicare will reimburse. It assumes that decreased federal spending will still satisfy the health care needs of the land. Someone, however, will have to pay for the health care of those removed from the Medicaid lists and for the services that are no longer reimbursed. Someone, somewhere, gets stuck with the bill. Instead of achieving cost containment, this method achieves cost shifting.

A similar practice has led the Health Insurance Association of America to estimate that in 1982 $5.8 billion in charges were shifted from government sources to private patients. The association further estimated that continuing government cutbacks could cause this figure to double by 1985. In anticipation of that day private insurers have already trimmed benefits and raised premiums by 20–40 percent. Cost shifting is thus not true cost containment because overall spending continues to escalate regardless of who pays.

Another federal idea that has come and gone is legislative coercion. On two separate occasions President Jimmy Carter attempted to put ceilings on total national capital expenditures for health care facilities and to restrict Medicare and Medicaid increases. Even if he had succeeded, most observers believe that the implementing legislation would have simply led to a diminution of services for the poor and disadvantaged.

Government regulations requiring health facilities to apply for a certificate of need prior to significant purchases or expenditures also have often not had the desired effect. After some hospitals were unable to justify their purchase of a CT scanner, it was found that they spent more money transporting their patients to a neighboring scanner than they would have spent purchasing their own. Only in the short term are costs cut in this manner.

The most recent federal strategy, which went into effect October 1983, incorporates capital cutbacks as well as controls in its concept of "diagnostic related groups," or prospective payment, for hospitals treating Medicare patients. Payment is based on diagnosis regardless of what services the patient actually receives. It is still too early to decide whether the new system will reward efficient facilities or rather those who learn how to provide quick cheap care of questionable quality.

If the predominant wind of change is cost containment, not far behind is an underwriting system based on prepayment and risk sharing. The system is in a sense a cost-shifting mechanism that transfers the bulk of the burden from the sick to the population as a whole. The concept implies, as any insurance idea does, that it is better for the many to pay for the few rather than for the unfortunate few to bankrupt themselves paying for themselves. Prepayment further assumes that with the money already collected before anyone gets sick it is in everyone's best interest to keep people out of hospitals insofar as that is feasible. The increased number of HMOs in the 1970s was the one concrete expression of this concept.

Most developed nations have decided that prepayment or entitlement for the entire population is the most effective tool in controlling health care costs. In Great Britain, for example, such a system costs only 5.5 percent of the GNP. However, by common consensus, quality in that system is in question, while a parallel private provider system for those who can afford to pay is thriving. In Canada a total of 8 percent of the GNP is spent on the various prepayment systems run by the provinces, and there is some question whether their 2 percent savings compared to the U.S. cost is worth the trouble.

Whatever its merits or deficiencies, some sort of universal

prepayment scheme seems to be a future probability for this country. It seems equally certain that any entity already capturing thirty-three cents of every health dollar and employing millions of people—that is, the MIC companies—must be woven into any new system. I envision, then, the possibility of a federally administered cost-effective system underwritten by a prepayment mechanism involving the corporations of the MIC, Blue Cross, and a Kaiser-type entity. But before such a confederation can take place, several things will have to happen:

**1. Recognition by the federal government of the strengths of the MIC.** The tremendous capital resources coupled with the corporate know-how and efficiency of the MIC must be recognized and tapped. The ability of the MIC to bring health care services to previously underserved communities must be taken advantage of. Also, its bottom-line hard-nosed financial attitude can be useful as a counterbalance to the wasteful attitudes of almost all other parties.

**2. Recognition of the weaknesses of the MIC.** Most of the MIC corporations have not accepted the fact that there is a difference between medical suppliers and medical providers. In the interest of all, facilities that deliver health care should not be permitted to also manufacture and sell pills and medical necessities to these same patients. The MIC companies cannot expect general acceptance until they and their directors conform to accepted health care standards, much as they expect their physicians to practice in conformity with accepted community standards. They must also accept the reality that their hospitals cannot all be located in suburban areas catering only to the white-collar country club crowd.

**3. The MIC must be brought into the mainstream of the health care system.** Serious cooperative efforts between the MIC companies and the government must commence. At the very least a dialogue should be undertaken between the MIC and the Department of Health and Human Services to explore areas of joint responsibility. Moreover, a willingness must be shown on the part of medical schools to involve proprietary hospitals in teaching. The arrangement would have the dual effect of injecting some youthful idealism and medical ethics into the MIC and at the same time allowing the "ivory towers" to understand these corporate giants. At present little communication exists between the two.

The MIC companies must realize that it is not necessary to buy out the medical profession in order to run hospitals. They must begin to work within the traditional medical channels and develop communication with county medical societies in their communities. Friction between proprietary hospital administrations and their medical staffs is a waste of time and energy. Physicians need hospital beds and hospitals need physicians.

The corporations must come to realize that health care is a service with a long tradition of going the extra mile. The MIC must learn to give back something to the communities and the health care system as a whole; up until now the MIC has been a taker. Hospital Corporation of America's recent unsuccessful bid to buy the Harvard-affiliated McLean Hospital strikes the right chord—though there were many physicians, to be sure, who looked at the proposal with some skepticism.

To propose a cooperative effort between government and the MIC is not novel or radical. NASA put a man on the moon in a joint venture with private industry, and the Pentagon has built many an awesome machine together with industry. In simple terms government has the power while the corporations have the money and the know-how.

Everyone—government, the MIC, and the medical profession—will have to give a little in order to work together for the common good. The rewards for a cooperative effort could be great for all concerned. Failure to work together could prove catastrophic. The MIC is as dependent and vulnerable

191

as any other entity. There will be no point to owning hospitals and selling pills if there is no money to pay the bills.

Despite the sometimes harsh remarks I've made in this book, I am convinced that the MIC must be an integral part of any future cost-effective system. I doubt that all its profits will continue to grow in this new era, but in order to survive it will have to participate. I would hope that some of the criticisms will be accepted in a constructive sense. In a way I look upon this book as a commencement of a positive dialogue.

It is important too that the American public itself become more knowledgeable concerning the health care system. A massive shift of resources from the curative side to the preventive will have to be achieved in order to realistically cut costs. The public will have to be educated about the destructive aspects of overutilization. Courses in health care should find their way into the country's schools and colleges. If America would eat, drink, and smoke less while exercising more, billions of dollars could be saved. The public agencies should disseminate information on new medical procedures such as coronary bypass, indicating their pros and cons. In short, we must work toward the goal of converting every American from a wasteful spender to a prudent buyer.

In 1974 Marc LaLonde, then the Canadian minister of National Health and Welfare, proposed a radical redirection of government funds from curative to preventive programs. His ideas gained some prominence at the time, but to date little has been accomplished. The concept, ten years ahead of its time then, is timely now.

In such a possible shift of emphasis, public education ought to concentrate on the simple maladies of everyday life. While the media zeroes in on the millions being spent on flashy life-saving procedures such as heart and liver transplants, billions more are quietly wasted on mundane illnesses such as the flu or indigestion. The medical journals are full of articles agonizing on the subject of who shall live and who shall die when expensive procedures are rationed, while the really big money is spent on treating the common cold at emergency rooms across the country. It has been estimated that if half the people with the common cold who seek medical advice were to care for themselves, $25 billion could have been saved each year, and that is probably a conservative estimate.

Physicians themselves have learned something about disease prevention. The age-standardized death rate for American white male physicians is 75 percent of that for all white males; and the rate for American white female physicians is 84 percent of that for all white females. It has been found that physicians as a group smoke less, drink less, exercise more, and are leaner than the population as a whole. The findings are not related merely to educational attainment or socioeconomic status; lawyers, for example, do not have the same healthful habits.

There are serious voices that claim we should not tinker with our superb health care system. After all, they argue, the average American life-span since 1960 has increased from sixty-eight to seventy-four years and infant mortality has dropped in the same period from 26.1 to 12.5 for every 1,000 births. These feats have been achieved by paying our bills and by reimbursing doctors and hospitals whatever they charge. But to a large degree we have been insulated from the true costs by government and insurance companies. As that insulation gets stripped away by increasing premiums and decreasing government spending, the "laissez-faire" advocates are decreasing in numbers. In simple terms the entire system is on the verge of defaulting. The trick, of course, is to prevent default and maintain the superb quality of American health care.

In the words of Eli Ginzberg of Columbia University, we need "a reduced inflow of real resources into the health care system without a diminution in useful output that would

193

adversely affect the satisfaction of patients or their health status." The system itself must work toward the goal so eloquently expressed by a resolution made at the thirtieth World Health Assembly in May 1977:

> *The main social target . . . in the coming decades should be the attainment by all citizens of the world by the year 2000 of a level of health that will permit them to lead a socially and economically productive life.*

The message to the mediglomerate corporations is clear. Profits are still attainable within the confines of cost containment and both are compatible with the lofty goal of quality treatment for every human being.

# BIBLIOGRAPHY

## BOOKS AND ARTICLES

Abelson, A. Up and Down Wall St. *Barron's,* 17 October 1983: 1,59.

Aday, L.A., and Anderson, R. *Development of indices of access to medical care.* Ann Arbor, Mich: Health Administration Press, 1975.

Alsop, R. After a slow start, Du Pont pushes harder for a bigger share of pharmaceutical sales. *Wall Street Journal,* 16 June 1983:31.

Altman, S.H., and Blendon, R., eds. Medical technology: The culprit behind health care costs? Publication (PHS) 79-3216. Washington: U.S. Department of Health, Education and Welfare, 1979.

AMA Insights. The inflation rate for physicians' services. *Journal of the American Medical Association (JAMA).* 249 (1983):3296.

Anderson, R., Kravits, J., and Anderson, O.W. *Equity in health services.* Bollinger Publishing Co., 1975.

Applied Management Sciences Inc. *An analysis of determinants health care utilization.* Silver Springs, Md.: AMS, 1980.

Banta D. Computed tomography: cost containment misdirected. *American Journal of Public Health* 70 (1980):215-16.

Binker, J.P., Mostellar, C.F., and Barnes, B.A. *Costs, risks, and benefits of surgery.* New York: Oxford University Press, 1977.

Blendon, J.B., and Rogers, D.E. Cutting medical care costs. *JAMA* 250 (1983):1880-85.

Blumenthal, D., Feldman, P., and Zeckhouser, R. Misuse of technology: a system not the disease, in McNeil, B.J., and Crovalno, E.G., eds.: *Critical issues in medical technology.* Boston: Auburn House, 1982:163-74.

Brown, L.D. Competition and cost containment: cautions and conjectures. *Milbank Mem Fund Q* 59 (1981):145-89.

Burleson-Macintyre. Plan National Health Act.

Califano, J.A., Jr. *Governing America: An insiders report from the White House and Cabinet.* New York: Simon & Schuster, 1981:136-71.

Caper, P. Competition and health care: A new Trojan horse. *N Engl J Med* 306 (1982):928-29.

Conn, R.B. Clinical laboratories: profit center, production industry or patient-care resource? *N Engl J Med* 298 (1978):422-27.

Connelly, D., and Steele, B. Laboratory utilization problems and solutions. *Arch Pathol Lab Med* 104 (1980):59-62.

Cooper, A. Restrictive covenants. *JAMA* 248 (1982):3091-92.

Cottrell, J.J., et al. Critical care computing. *JAMA* 248 (1982):2269-91.

Davis, K. *National health insurance: benefits, costs, and sequences.* Washington, D.C.: Brookings Institution, 1975:9–11.

Dellums Bill, Health Rights Act.

Ekaterini, S. *Investor owned hospitals and their role in changing health care.* New York: F&S Press, 1981.

Dismuke, S.E., and Miller, S.T. Why not share the secrets of good health? The physicians role in health promotion. *JAMA* 249 (1983):3181–83.

Donald, C.A., et al. Conceptualization and measurement of health for adults in the health insurance survey. Publication R-1987/4-HEW (vol. 4). Santa Monica, Calif.: Rand Corporation, 1978.

Expensive medical technologies. Editorial, *Lancet* 1 (1983):279–80.

Eisenberg, B.S. Medical practice expenses: Trends, determinants and impact, National Commission on the cost of health care, 1976–1977. *JAMA* 2 (1978):37–60.

Enthoven Proposals, Consumer Choice Health Plans (CCHP).

Evans, W.E. Health care technology and the inevitability of resource and rationing decisions, part I. *JAMA* 249 (1983):2047–53.

Evans, W.E. Health care technology and the inevitability of resource allocation and rationing decisions, part II. *JAMA* 249 (1983):2206–19.

Fein, R. Effects of cost sharing in health insurance: A call for caution. *N Engl J Med.* 305 (1981):1526–28.

Feldstein, M.S. An economic model of the Medicare system. *Quarterly Journal of Economics* 85 (1971):1–20.

Feldstein, M. Hospital costs and health insurance. Cambridge, Mass: Harvard University Press, 1981.

Fetter, R.B., Shin, Y. and Freeman, G.L. Case mix definition of diagnosis-related groups. *Medical Care* 18 (1980): Suppl. 1–53.

Fisher, C.R. Differences by age groups in health care spending. *Health Care Finance Review* 1 (1980):66–90.

Friedman, M. Capitalism and freedom. Chicago: Phoenix Books, 1962:149–60.

Frist, T.F., Jr. A cottage industry no more. *The Internist* 23 (10) (1983):8–9.

Fuchs, V.R. The battle for control of health care. *Stanford MD,* Winter 1983:2–5.

Fulton Duncan Bill, Comprehensive Health Care Insurance Act.

Gibson, R., and Waldo, D.R. National health expenditures, 1980. *Health Care Financing Review* September (1981).

Ginzberg, E. Cost containment imaginary and real. *N Engl J Med* 308 (1983):1220–23.

Glaser, W.A. Paying the hospital: Foreign lessons for the U.S. New York: Columbia University Center for the Social Sciences, 1982.

Hadley, J. *More medical care, better health?* Washington, D.C.; The Urban Institute Press, 1982.

Hager, M. $290 billion a year and growing. *Consumers Digest,* May, June (1983):10–50.

Hamburger, S. Cost-effective medicare care. *JAMA* 249 (1983):3302.

Healthy people. The surgeon general's report on health promotion and disease prevention. VII-X (DHEW) publication no. (PHS) 79-55071. Washington, D.C.: Department of Health, Education and Welfare, 1979.

Herrell, J.H. Health care expenditures: The approaching crisis. *Mayo Clinic Proceedings* 55 (1980):705-10.

Hill, A.B. *Principles of medical statistics.* New York: Oxford University Press, 1971.

Hirsh, B.D. Antitrust and professional activities. *JAMA* 250 (1983):491-92.

Iglehart, J.K. Medicare's uncertain future. *N Engl J Med* 306 (1982):1308-12.

Iglehart, J.K. The new era of prospective payment for hospitals. *N Engl J Med* 307 (1982):1288-92.

Javitz Bill, National Health Insurance and Health Services Improvement Act.

Jellinek, P.S. Medical cost inflation. *N Engl J Med* 307 (1982):1649-50.

————. Yet another look at medical cost inflation. *N Engl J Med* 307 (1982):496-97.

Keeler, E.B., and Rolph, J.E. How cost sharing reduced medical spending of participants in the health insurance experiment. *JAMA* 249 (1983):2220-22.

Kennedy-Corman Bill, Health and Security Act of 1975.

Klarman, H.E. Application of cost-benefit analysis to the health services and the special care of technologic innovation. *Int J Health Sen* 4 (1974):325-52.

Kleinfield, N.R. New approach to health care: N.M.E. helps alter pattern, analysts say. *New York Times,* 19 July 1983:27–30.

Kleinfield, N.R. Operating for profit at Hospital Corporation. *New York Times,* 29 May 1983: Sec. 3, 1–22.

Kleinfield, N.R. The king of the HMO mountain. *New York Times,* Sec. 3:L, 31 July 1983.

Lalonde, M. A new perspective on the health of Canadians: A working document. Ottawa: Information Canada, 1975:5–6.

Lashoff, J.C., et al. The role of cost-benefit and cost-effectiveness analysis in controlling health care costs, in McNeil, B.J., and Cravalho, E.G., eds.: *Critical issues in medical technology.* Boston: Auburn House, 1982.

Le Maitre, G.D. Medical cost inflation. *N Engl J Med* 307 (1982):1649.

Lee, B. Medical cost inflation. *N Engl J Med* 307 (1982):1649.

Levitan, M.S. Statement of the Association of American Medical Colleges before the National Council on Health Planning and Development. Washington, D.C.: Association of American Medical Colleges, 8 March 1982.

Lewin, L.S., Derzon, R.A., and Margulies, R. Investor-owned and nonprofits differ in economic performance. *Hospitals* 55(13):52–58 (1981).

Long–Ribicoff Catastrophic Insurance and Medical Assistance Act.

Luft, H.S. How do health maintenance organizations achieve their "savings?" rhetoric and evidence. *N Engl J Med* 298 (1978):1336–43.

Luft, H.L., Bunker, J.P., and Enthoven, A.C. Should operations be regionalized? *N Engl J Med* 301 (1979):364–69.

Marx, J.L., and Hauser, M.R. *The med tech directory.* South Orange, N.J.: Med Tech Services, Inc., 1982.

McCarthy, E.G., and Finkel, M.L. Surgical utilization in the U.S.A. *Med Care* 18 (1980):883–91.

Mechanic, D. *Medical sociology,* 2d ed. New York: Free Press, 1978.

Mechanic, D. The growth of medical technology and bureaucracy: implications for medical care. *Milbank Mem Fund Q* 55 (1977):61–78.

Merry, R.W., and Schoor, B. Medicare fund crisis may spur competition in health care fields. *Wall Street Journal,* 29 June 1983.

Moore, T. Way out front in nursing homes. *Fortune,* 13 June 1983: 142–50.

National HMO Census. Annual report on the growth of HMOs in the U.S., 1982. Interstudy, Excelsior, Minn.: Interstudy, 1983.

Newhouse, J.P. A design for a health insurance experiment. *The Inquiry* 11 (1974):5–27.

————. Some interim results from a controlled trial of cost sharing in health insurance. *N Engl J Med* 305 (1981):1501–07.

Newport, J.P., Jr. The Fortune directory of the largest U.S. non-industrial corporations. *Fortune,* 13 June 1983: 153–76.

Office of Technology Assessment. The implications of cost-effectiveness: Analysis of medical technology. Washington, D.C.: Government Printing Office, 1980.

Ownes, A. How much of your money comes from third parties? *Med Econ* April (1983):254–63.

Pattison, R.V., and Katz, H.M. Investor-owned and not-for-profit hospitals. *N Engl J Med* 309 (1983):374–53.

Pear, R. Hospitals worry over fixed set for Medicare. *New York Times* 28 August 1983:1–20.

Peters, R.K., et al. Physical fitness and subsequent mycocardial infarction in healthy workers. *JAMA* 249 (1983):3052–56.

Phelps, C.E., and Newhouse, J.P. Coinsurance, the price of time and the demand for medical services. *Rev Econ Stat* 56 (1974):334–42.

Physicians Wanted Section. *JAMA* 248 (1982):2392–99.

Positions Available Section. *JACEP* 11 (1982):90–100.

Prescription for Profits. *Time,* 4 July 1983:42–43.

Reinhold, R. Majority in survey on health care are open to changes to cut costs. *New York Times,* 29 March 1982:a1 (col.3).

Relman, A.S. Investor-owned hospitals and health-care costs. *N Engl J Med* 309 (1983):370–72.

————. Speech at annual meeting of National Electrical Manufacturers Association, September 21, 1982.

————. The new medical-industrial complex. *N Engl J Med* 303 (1980):936–70.

Renne, K.S. Measurement of social health in general population survey. *Social Sci Res* 3 (1974):24–44.

Rice, D.P. Estimating the cost of illness. Public Health Service Publication 947–6. Washington, D.C.: Government Printing Office, 1966.

Robinson, D. Investor-owned hospitals: RX for success. *Reader's Digest,* April 1983:82–86.

Rooney, A.A. *A few minutes with Andy Rooney.* New York: Warner Books, 1982.

Rosenberg, C.L. Payment by diagnosis: How the great experiment is going. *Med Econ* 59 (May 10, 1982):245–57.

Rudnitsky, H., and Konrad, W. Trouble in the elysian fields. *Forbes* 29 August 1983:58–59.

Russell, T. How much does medical technology cost? *Bull N Y Acad Med* 54 (1978):124–32.

Schweiker, R. Budget Report to Congress from Secretary of Health and Human Services. Washington, D.C.: U.S. Government Printing Office, December 1982.

Seen, M. Fishing for a forum on health policy. 219 (1983):37–38.

Sellers, T. Non-24-hour clinics should eschew "emergency." *Emergency Dept News* 15 (1982):2.

Sloan, F.A., and Vraciu, R.A. Investor-owned and not-for-profit hospitals: addressing some issues. *Health Affairs* (Spring 1983):25–27.

Sorenson, L. Hospitals and doctors compete for patients with rising bitterness. *Wall Street Journal,* 19 July 1983:1.

Standard & Poor's. *Monthly Reports.* 1982, 1983.

Starr, P. *The social transformation of American medicine.* New York: Basic Books, 1982.

Statistical Profile of the Investor-Owned Industry, 1981. Washington, D.C.: Federation of American Hospitals, 1981.

Stockman, D.A. Premises for a medical marketplace: A neoconservative vision of how to transform the health system. *Health Affairs* 1(1981):5–18.

Stoddart, G.L., and Barer, M.L. Analysis of demand for utilization through episodes of medical service, in Van der Gaay, J., and Perlman, M., eds., *Health, economics, and health economics*. New York: Elsevier North Holland Inc., 1981:149–70.

Studies in the comparative performance of investor-owned and not-for-profit hospitals. Industry Analysis, vol. 1. Washington, D.C.: Levin and Associates, Inc., 1981.

Studies in the comparative performance of investor-owned and not-for-profit hospitals, vol. 4. *The comparative economic performance of a matched sample of investor-owned and not-for-profit hospitals*. Washington, D.C.: Levin and Associates, Inc., 1981.

Suber, D.G., and Tabor, W.J. Withholding of life-sustaining treatment for the terminally ill, incompetent patient: who decides? *JAMA* 248 (1982):2250–51.

Tax Equity and Fiscal Responsibility Act, 1983: TEFKA; PL 97–248.

The upheaval in health care. Cover Story, *Business Week*, 25 July 1983:44–56.

Trauner, J., and Luft, H. Entrepreneurial trends in health care delivery: the developmental of retail dentistry and freestanding ambulatory services. Washington, D.C.: Federal Trade Commission, Washington Memo, 7 January 1983.

Ulman Bill; National Health Care Services Reorganization Act.

U.S. Bureau of the Census. America's elderly in the 1980s. Washington, D.C.: Population Reference Bureau Publication, 1981.

U.S. Department of Commerce. Statistical Abstract of the United States. Washington, D.C.: Bureau of the Census, 1980.

U.S. Department of Health and Human Services. Report of Inspector General, October 1983. Washington, D.C.

U.S. General Accounting Office. Primer on competitive strategies for containing health care costs. Washington, D.C.: GAO, 1981; HRD 89–92.

U.S. General Accounting Office. Improving Medicare and Medicaid systems to control payments for unnecessary physicians services. Washington, D.C.: A#120544 (GAO/HRD-83-16); 8 August 1983.

U.S. National Center for Health Statistics. Current estimates from the health interview survey. Services 10;136. Washington, D.C.: Department of Health and Human Services, April 1981.

Winans, R.F. Analysts warn that many health-care stocks trade more on their promise than on reality. *Wall Street Journal,* 16 June 1983:53.

Wong, E.T., McCarron, M.M, and Shaw, S.T., Jr. Ordering of laboratory tests in a teaching hospital. *JAMA* 249 (1983):3076–80.

World Health Organization. *Handbook of resolutions and decisions of the World Health Assembly and the Executive Boom.* 4th ed., vol 2 (1973–80).

Wright, R.A., and Allen, B.H. Marketing and medicine: Why advertising is not an issue. *JAMA* 250 (1983):47–48.

Wyden, R. Preferred Provider Health Care Act. Bill HR 2956. Washington, D.C.

Yale–New Haven Hospital. *Report to the Commission on Hospitals and Health Care on the Joint Study.* New Haven, Conn: Yale–New Haven Hospital, April 1981.

Young, Arthur & Co. Health care briefing: May 2 (1982).

———. Health care briefing: 6:May 2 (1983).

———. Health care focus: Roundtable 1983: Multi-institutional service strategies: 8:1–16 (March/April 1983).

## HOSPITAL DATA

*American Hospital Association hospital statistics* (1980 ed.). Chicago: American Hospital Association, 1980.

*California Hospital Association News:* 29 October 1982.

Duckett, S. J., and Kristofferson, S. M. An index of hospital performance. *Medical Care* 16 (1978): 400–7.

Washington Memo 2/14/83: Bureau of Health Professions; Department of Health and Human Services.

Ebert, R. H.; and Brown, S. S. Academic health centers. *N Engl J Med* 308 (1983): 1200–8.

Gross, M. E. W.; and Reed, J. I. Evaluating the quality of hospital care through severity-adjusted death rates. *Medical Care* 12 (1974): 202–13.

Hebel, J. R., et al. Assessment of hospital performance by use of death rates. *JAMA* 248 (1982):3131–35.

Lee, J.A.H.; Morrison, S. L.; and Morris, G. N. Case fatality in teaching and non-teaching hospitals. *Lancet* 1 (1960): 170–71.

Mason, W. B., et al. Why people are hospitalized: A description of preventable factors leading to admission for medical illness. *Medical Care* 18 (1980): 147–63.

Roemer, M. J.; Moustafa, A.T.; and Hopkins, C.E. A proposed hospital quality index. Hospital death rates adjusted for COD severity. *Health Serv Res* 3 (1968): 96–118.

Rosenberg, C. L. Your own hospital may be your toughest competitor. *Med Econ* 6 (1982):154–64.

## HISTORICAL DATA

Cabot, R. C. *A guide to the clinical examination of the blood.* New York: William Wood and Co., 1897.

King, L. S. Clinical laboratories become important, 1870–1900. *JAMA* 249 (1983): 3025–29.

Mills, C. W. *White collar.* New York: Oxford University Press, 1951.

Osler, W. *Aequanimitas.* New York: McGraw-Hill, 1906.

## PHYSICIAN DATA

*ACEP News.* American College of Emergency Physicians, 1983; special ed., May 1983.

*AMA Insights.* Primary care physicians numbered in AMA physician masterfile. *JAMA* 249 (1983):2005-2006.

Brashaw, J. S. *Doctors on trial.* New York: Paddington Press, 1978.

Davis, K. Implications of an expanding supply of physicians. *Johns Hopkins Medical Jounal* 150 (1982):55-64.

Fuchs, V. R. The supply of surgeons and the demand for operations. *Journal of Human Resources* 1978; 13 suppl: 35-36.

Fuchs, V. R., and Kramer, M. Determinants of expenditures for physicians services in the U.S., 1948-1968. Publication HSM 73-3013. Washington, D.C.: National Center for Health Services Research and Development, 1972.

Health Policy Center. Analysis of survey data on physician practice costs and incomes. Nashville, Tenn.: Vanderbilt University, Institute for Public Policy Studies, 1981.

Hemenway, D. The optimal location of doctors. *N Engl J Med* 306 (1982):397-401.

Jonsen, A. R. Watching the doctor. *N Engl J Med* 308 (1983): 1531-35.

King, L. S. The old code of medical ethics and some problems it had to face. *JAMA* 248 (1982):2329-32.

Sloan, F. A., and Schwartz, W. B. Physician income as supply expands. *JAMA* 249 (1983):766-69.

Tarlov, A. R. The increasing supply of physicians, the changing structure of the health services system, and the future practice of medicine. *N Engl J Med* 308 (1983):1235-44.

# ANNUAL REPORTS (1981, 1982) AND 10K FINANCIAL ANNUAL REPORTS TO SECURITIES AND EXCHANGE COMMISSION (1981, 1982)

ADAC Laboratories

ARA Services

Acme United Corporation

Affiliated Hospital Products, Inc.

Alo-Scherer Healthcare

Alza Corporation

American Diagnostics

American Hospital Supply

American Medical Buildings

American Medical International

American Medi-Dent, Inc.

American Sterilizer

American Surgery Centers

American Vision Centers

Apple Computer

Bard (C. R.)

Bausch & Lomb, Inc.

Baxter Travenol

Becton, Dickinson and Company

Beecham Group

Benedict Nuclear Pharmacy, Inc.

Berkeley Bio-Medical, Inc.

Beverly Enterprises

Blue Cross of Northern California. Annual Report, 1981.

Blue Cross of California. Annual Report, 1982.

Bio Logicals, Inc.

Bio-Medicus, Inc.

Biochem International

Biotech Capital Corporation

Bristol-Myers

Care Centers, Inc.

Care Corporation

Cetus Corporation

Charter Medical

Collagen Corporation

Community Psychiatric Centers

Concept, Inc.

Connecticut General Insurance

Damon Corporation

Datascope Corporation

Del Laboratories

Delmed, Inc.

Diagnostic Products

Dow Chemical Company

Ealing Corporation

Eastman Kodak Company

Electromedics, Inc.

Foremost-McKesson

Genentech

General Electric

HBO & Company

Hazleton Laboratories

Health Care Fund

Healthdyne, Inc.

Hewlett-Packard

Hospital Corporation of America

Humana, Inc.

Huntington Health Services

Hybritech

ICN Pharmaceuticals

IMMutron

INA Corporation

INA Investment Securities

International Business Machines

Johnson & Johnson

Laser Industries

Lifemark Corporation

Lilly (Eli)

Long's Drug Stores

Marian Laboratories

Merck & Company

National Medical Care

National Medical Enterprises

Neo-Bionics

Pfizer, Inc.

Scherer (RP) Corporation

Scientific Leasing, Inc.

Searle (G. D.)

Sears, Roebuck

Squibb Corporation

Sterling Drug, Inc.

Stryker Corporation

Sybron Corporation

Syntex Corporation

Temp-Stick Corporation

Teva Pharmaceuticals Ltd.

Thompson Medical

Tyco Laboratories

United Medical Corporation

Vari-Care, Inc.

Whitman Medical
    Corporation

# ACKNOWLEDGMENTS

This book began life as an idea in the mind of the late Hugh Cohen, and it owes its subsequent tangible existence to his continual help and encouragement while I went about writing it. Hugh, for many years an account executive with a Wall Street securities firm, also opened many otherwise locked doors for me and filled my study with reams of pertinent and significant data. His razor-sharp reasoning and keen understanding proved invaluable as I struggled with the intricacies of conglomerate and mediglomerate anatomy. More important, Hugh was a kind and gentle man and, to me, a devoted and loyal friend. His courageous battle with the disease that took his life while he was in his prime taught me what it is to have determination and resignation in the face of impossible odds. I have learned more from his example and his friendship than I can adequately acknowledge and I feel a greater gratitude to him than I know how to express.

Roz Siegel's enthusiastic direction helped transform my notes into a cohesive book. Morty Schiff edited the manuscript and also served in many instances as my sounding board and reality tester, and I gratefully thank him.

Jack Graudenz put up with me and my questions day in and day out for five years, which is how long it took the book to evolve. As busy as he was as chief executive officer of a San

Francisco mediglomerate, he always made the time to help me crystallize my thoughts and order my ideas. He also supplied me with, when necessary, a computer, a word processor, and a library of data bases. I fell back upon his profound knowledge of the health care field and his mastery of computer software many times in the course of writing, and I am deeply grateful to him.

Isaac Schiff, a friend since boyhood and now an eminent physician and surgeon, also took the time to listen to some of my wilder notions and returned them to me after having separated the significant and true among them from the extravagant and dubious.

JoAnn Richardson waded through hundreds of pages of manuscript written in an atrocious handwriting as she typed version after version of the work. She also coordinated the technical aspects of the project, and I am truly grateful to her.

Other good and talented friends read the manuscript in its various stages of completion and made many useful and important suggestions. For all their help I warmly thank them.

My wife, Arlene, and my children, David, Philip, and Michelle, dutifully tolerated all my excesses during the many manic months devoted to the actual writing of the book. Their love and support, which I reciprocate anew ahere, saw me through the roughest times and ultimately made, for me, the entire project both possible and worthwhile.

# INDEX